A Windows NT™ Guide to the Web

Springer Science+Business Media, LLC

Richard Raucci

A Windows NT™
Guide to the Web

Covering browsers, servers, and related software

With 125 Illustrations

Springer

Richard Raucci
435 Eureka Street
San Francisco, CA 94114 USA
rraucci@well.com
rraucci@interramp.com
http://www.well.com/Community/rraucci/raucci.html

Windows NT is a trademark of Microsoft Corporation. Microsoft, Windows, Windows 95, and Visual Basic are registered trademarks of Microsoft Corporation.
Netscape and Netscape Navigator are trademarks of Netscape Communications Corporation.
SunSoft Workshop is a registered trademark of Sun Microsystems, Inc. Java and JavaScript are trademarks of Sun Microsystems, Inc.
NCSA Mosaic is a registered trademark of the National Center for Supercomputer Applications at the University of Illinois, Urbana-Champaign.
NextStep is a registered trademark of NeXT Software, Inc. WebObjects is a trademark of NeXT Software, Inc.
Informix is a registered trademark of Informix Software, Inc.
Oracle is a registered trademark of Oracle Corporation.
PowerPC is a registered trademark of International Business Machines Corporation.
PostScript is a registered trademark of Adobe Systems Incorporated. TIFF is a trademark of Adobe Systems Incorporated.
Intel is a registered trademark of Intel Corporation.

Library of Congress Cataloging-in-Publication Data
Raucci, Richard.
          A Windows NT guide to the web : covering browsers, servers, and
     related software / Richard Raucci.
              p. cm.
          Includes bibliographical references and index.
          ISBN 978-0-387-94792-1 (softcover : alk. paper)
          1. World Wide Web (Information retrieval system)
     2. Microsoft Windows NT I. Title.
     TK5105.888.R38 1997
     005.7'13–dc20   96-35818

Printed on acid-free paper.

© 1997 by Springer Science+Business Media New York
Originally published by Springer-Verlag New York Berlin Heidelberg in 1997

Production managed by Bill Imbornoni; manufacturing supervised by Jacqui Ashri.

9 8 7 6 5 4 3 2 1
SPIN 10539077

ISBN 978-0-387-94792-1   ISBN 978-1-4419-8572-9 (eBook)
DOI 10.1007/978-1-4419-8572-9

Contents

1
Introduction

NT as an Operating System

Microsoft developed Windows NT as an alternative to Unix. The company sees it as a part of its overall Enterprise Computing plan. It scales up from basic 486 systems to high-end RISC systems from companies like Digital, NEC, and PC vendors offering PowerPC systems for NT.

The basic operating system consists of a user interface shell (similar in appearance to Windows 3.1 for NT 3.1 to 3.5, and changing to look and feel more like Windows 95 for NT 4.0) designed to run 32-bit programs. This makes it ideal for the multimedia nature of Web browsers, and for the heavy-duty requirements of a Web server.

There are a number of elements in the OS that are special to NT. These include the control panels and administrative support tools relating to NT's services and support mechanisms. TCP/IP is included for Internet access through traditional networks. You can also connect from Windows NT Workstation via MS Remote Access to any Internet Access Provider supporting PPP.

Basic requirements for Windows NT Workstation are a 486 system with at least 8 MB of RAM, although 16 MB is recommended. The client software needed to connect to a corporate server is included, as is the Remote Access software mentioned earlier.

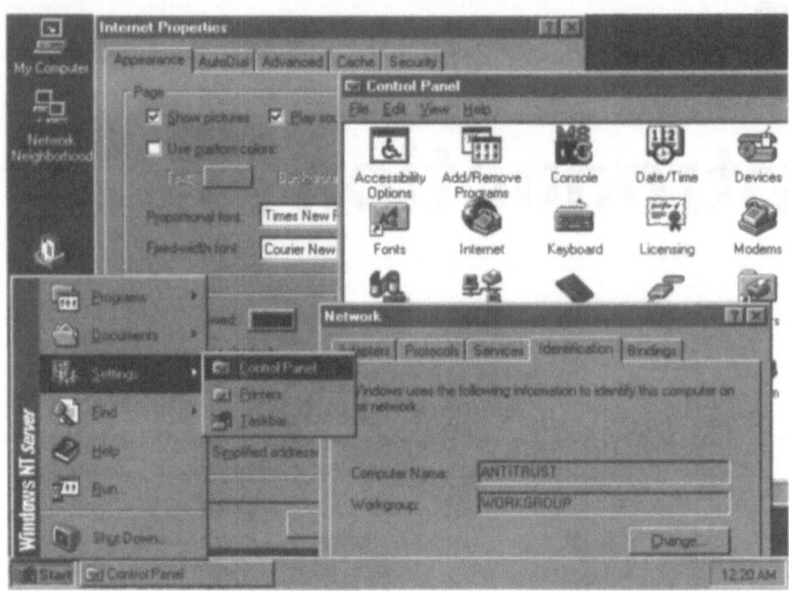

FIGURE 1.1.
NT 4.0 operating
system.

Basic requirements for Windows NT Server are a 486 system with 16 MB of RAM, preferably 32 MB. The cost of Pentium platforms is decreasing, so it's a good idea to bypass a 486, especially for a Web server, and go directly to a Pentium or Pentium Pro system.

NT Server 4.0 adds the Microsoft Internet Information Server as an integrated part of its software. It would be a good idea to explore whether you actually want to install this with your NT 4.0 installation and setup; many other Web servers for Windows NT exist, and some (like Netscape's) offer intrinsically better features.

Platforms for Windows NT

The Intel platform (486, Pentium, Pentium Pro) is the ubiquitous PC. NT Workstation scales down to the 486 platform, so you might consider upgrading PCs in your office environment to Windows NT instead of Windows 95, and enjoy a better-implemented 32-bit operating system.

NT also runs on MIPS RISC platforms from companies like NEC, and Digital Alpha 64-bit systems. These are high-end workstations that will usually cost more than PCs, but will deliver a higher degree of performance.

The PowerPC reference platform is a mid-range RISC system standard that is priced midway between common PCs and high-end workstations, and provides a good performance boost from the former. Some PC vendors are already offering PowerPC platforms with NT preinstalled at reasonable prices.

NT and Web Browsers

Because NT comes with networking software (both internal TCP/IP stacks and dial-up Remote Access), it's already set up to run Web browsers. The 32-bit nature of Windows NT means that it can run the most advanced Web browsers from companies like Netscape and Microsoft. These browsers can reach millions of Web pages across the Internet that feature a wide range of information on business subjects, computing, entertainment, finance, and much more.

A Web browser works with HTML (HyperText Markup Language) files, an Internet standard file type that describes how pictures, text, and audio files will combine into a multimedia document in your browser. Netscape and Internet Explorer support a wide range of file formats internally (with more being able to be added to Netscape 2.0 and 3.0 via plug-ins), and you can also add any alternate file type support to your Web browser via helper applications.

Helper Applications

Helper applications are those programs that allow Netscape to view images, play sound files, and run animations and movies. These can be configured quite easily from Netscape's Options/-Preferences panel (Fig. 1.2). Use the drop-down list to move to the Helper Applications section, and you can see a wide range of file formats that the Web browser already knows about.

The Helper Applications already preconfigured for use with Netscape are listed here. Use this as a guide to determine which ones you should download and install. Netscape's home page has links to the most common Helper Application Web and FTP sites; use it to configure the following applications. You can also find out about plug-ins for Navigator from the Netscape site.

Although Netscape already knows how to load certain image file formats natively, like JPEG and GIF files, other images at a Web site may be in different formats, like the TIFF image file format. You can use an external display program like LView to view these files externally. You can also use LView to view files

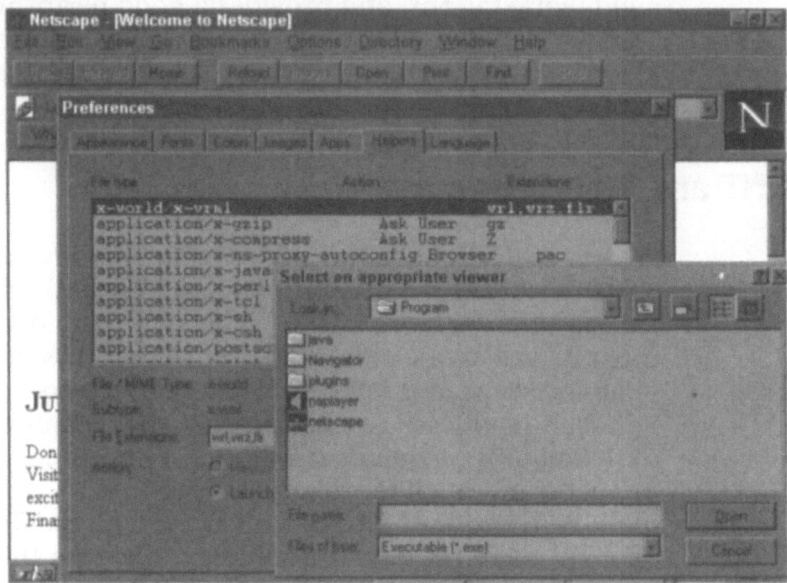

FIGURE 1.2.
Netscape's Options/
Preferences
Panel for Helper
Applications.

off-line that Netscape can handle internally, so you can continue to browse the Web site. Just download the file instead, and drag it on the LView icon. LView will also allow you to see formats like Windows' BMP and Mac PICT files. (See Fig. 1.3.)

The VMPEG program allows you to view MPEG animations and movies. You can find a version that will run with the WinG subsystem (for accelerated graphics) in the same release. VMPEG is available from the NT shareware sites listed in Chapter 4.

QuickTime is Apple's multimedia movie and animation protocol. Find out more about it at Apple's official QuickTime Web site, http://quicktime.apple.com. QuickTime for Windows is available for Windows NT at the QuickTime site.

Apple also recently developed QuickTimeVR (QTVR), a panoramic view QuickTime format for scenes that you can rotate through in three dimensions, and zoom in and out on. You'll need to load the QuickTimeVR player from Apple's Web site and set it as your QuickTime player in Netscape to make use of it (it will also play standard QuickTime movies). You can also download the QTVR movies and view them off-line using the QTVR Player.

Macromedia has made the Shockwave player available as a Netscape Navigator plug-in. It plays Director files inside your Web browser's main window, complex animations with sound support. You can find the plug-in at http://www.shockwave.com.

Use Netscape and Microsoft Internet Explorer's built-in sound support as a good, all-around audio player. Netscape is already

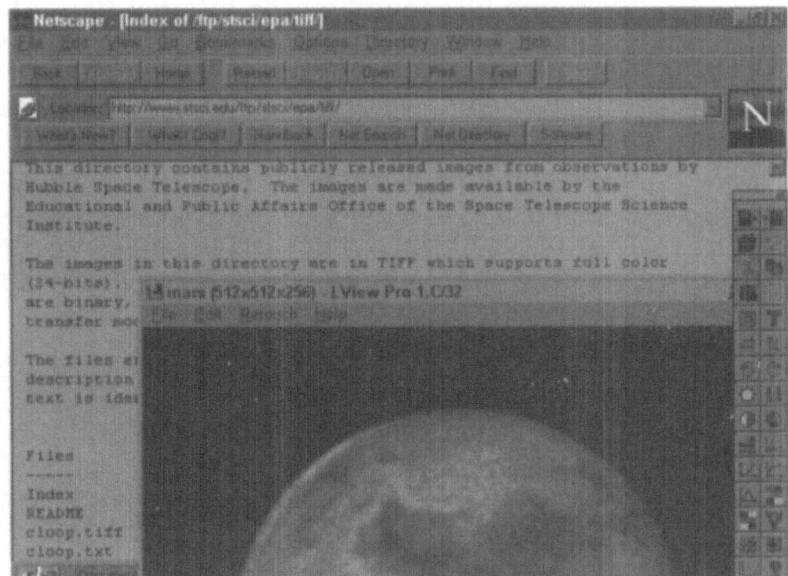

FIGURE 1.3.
LView launching an
external viewer.

FIGURE 1.4.
Netscape playing a
Shockwave file.

configured for it, and the program can handle standard PC.WAV
sound formats, as well as some of the more common formats
for sound files found on the Internet (the .AU and .AIFF types
especially). Microsoft Explorer plays sound files directly, while
Netscape uses a small helper application.

The RealAudio file format/application system allows you to
play audio files as they are downloading, instead of having to wait
through a long file transfer first. It's a significant development.
The player application automatically installs to Netscape's Preferences section as a Helper Application, and is very easy to set up.
You can find it at the RealAudio home page, http://www.realaudio
.com.

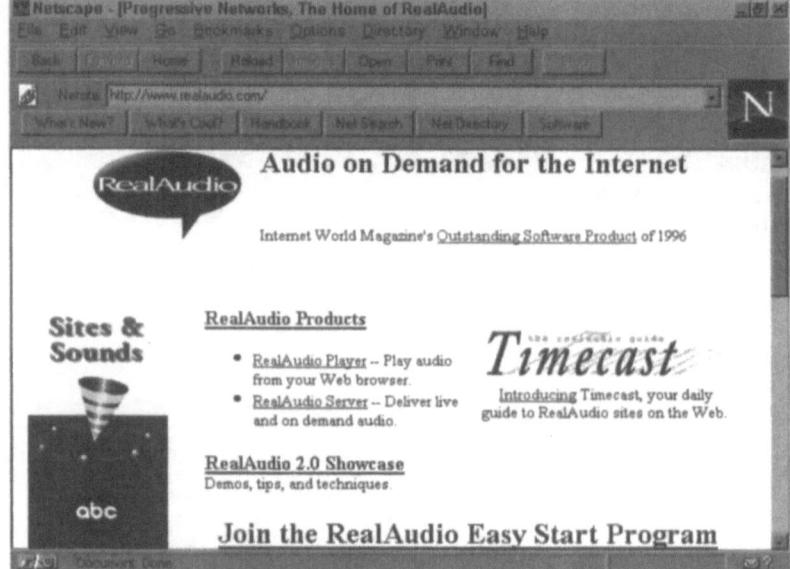

FIGURE 1.5.
The RealAudio Web
site.

Some files on the Internet will be in the PostScript format.
There are a number of ways that Netscape can handle these;
one of the easiest is to use an application like Adobe Illustrator
or Photoshop as a viewer. This can put a strain on your system
resources, however. There are also shareware PostScript viewers
in development, most notably Ghostscript. You can find out more
about it at the Ghostscript Web site, http://www.cs.wisc.edu:80/
~ghost/. The NT software is also available at http://www.ilex.
inter.net/gs.html. You can also use the Adobe Acrobat Distiller
application to convert the PostScript file to a PDF file you can
view using Acrobat Reader or Exchange. Note that all of these
techniques require configuring Netscape and other browsers to
use the alternate viewers.

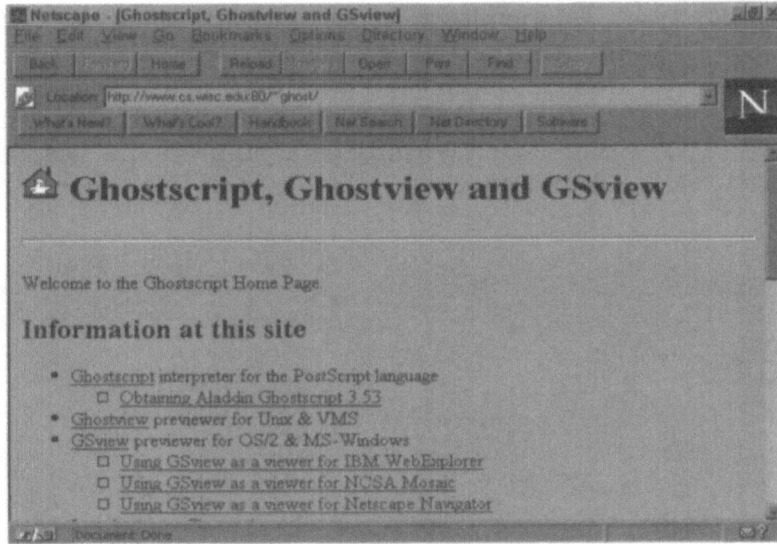

FIGURE 1.6.
The Ghostscript Web
site.

The Acrobat format mentioned above is a good way to get documents in their original format over the World Wide Web. You can download the Acrobat Reader program at no cost from Adobe (`http://www.adobe.com`), either as a direct plug-in for Netscape Navigator, or as an external program.

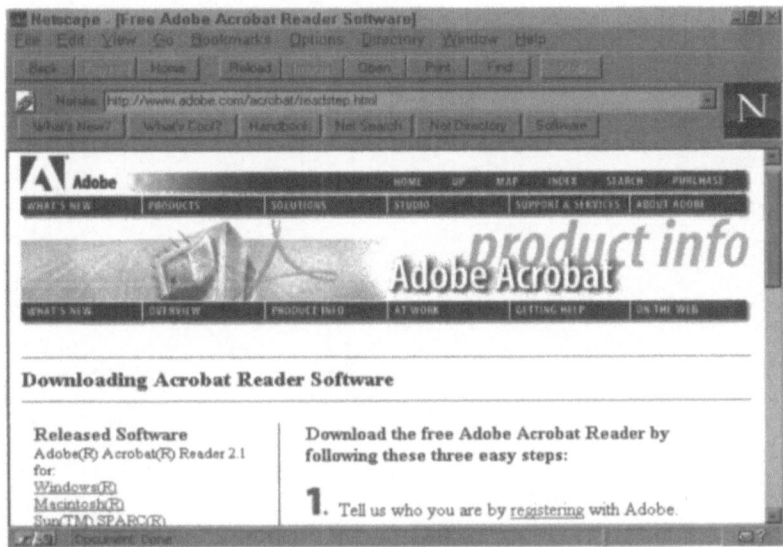

FIGURE 1.7.
Acrobat Reader
home page at the
Adobe Web site.

To download helper applications under Netscape, hold down the shift key while clicking on a file transfer link. Netscape will then save the file to your hard drive. The files will mostly be in a PKZip format, or a self-extracting archive. Use a shareware program called WinZip to decompress the files, then run its relevant setup programs.

2
Browsers for Windows NT and How to Get Connected

Your Web browsing experience will be significantly improved by choosing the proper browser. Microsoft is making a push to promote its own Internet Explorer, but Netscape Navigator still holds an edge. The National Center for Supercomputing Applications' Mosaic browser has fallen behind the front-runners, but still offers some unique features. For specialized environments, Oracle's PowerBrowser has strong connections to Oracle database applications, and the Alis Tango browser works in several different languages automatically.

Netscape Navigator 3.0

Netscape Navigator's main window is where you'll view Web pages. These are standard HTML files, composed of graphics and text that can also be linked to other Web documents. Navigator 3.0 is also capable of viewing in-line animation in the main window (Java files and GIF animations), and can view and play other types of media files directly by the use of in-line plug-ins, extensions to the main Netscape program.

Navigator 3.0 features a standard Windows file menu for accessing the program's main functions, plus an interactive toolbar for common Web-browsing activities. Below that, there's a location indicator that shows the Web address for the page you're currently viewing. You can also use a series of directory buttons to reach interesting Web indices located at Netscape's main Web site.

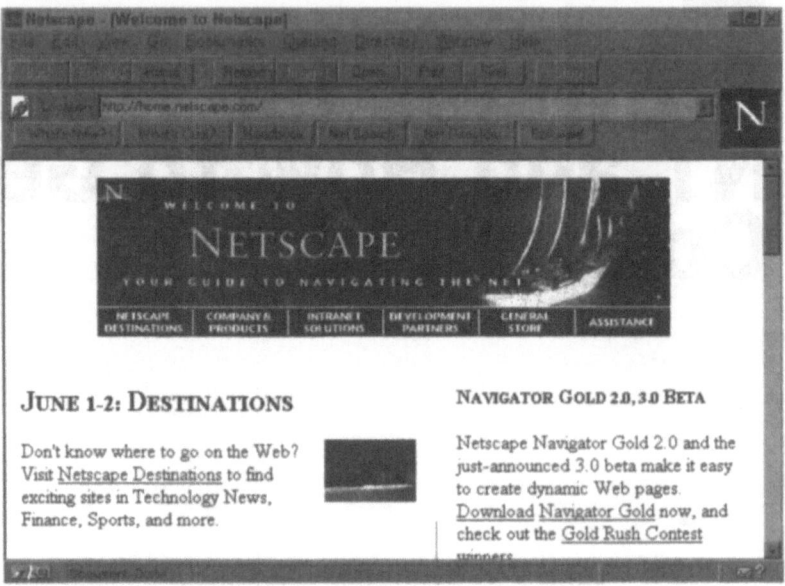

FIGURE 2.1.
Netscape main window.

The main window also has a progress bar you can use to track Web document transfers. To the left of the progress bar, there's a status line that will show different information on the current Web activities taking place. You can also use it to view link information. Just place your mouse pointer over a link, and the address will show in the bottom panel.

Under the File Menu, there are functions for launching new browsers and sending mail from your browser. The New Web Browser command will let you continue to use the Web while Netscape is downloading a page (Netscape supports multiple connections). The mail functions will let you pop up a mail window to send a quick message from your browser, or to mail a Web document or URL (either as an HTML attachment or as quoted text). The File Menu also has standard commands for opening a location (a Web URL) or a local file (HTML, images, and text), and for saving files that you've already loaded. You can also transmit a file via FTP from Netscape 2.0.

Use the Print commands to set up your printer, view a preview of how the Web page will print, and print it. Use the Close command to exit the current Netscape window; Exit will close the entire program.

The Edit Menu has standard commands for working with text (cut, copy, and paste commands), and a helpful Undo command.

You can use the Edit commands to highlight text in a Web page (even if it's not a link), and copy it to a local file (like Notepad). They're also helpful for copying and pasting URLs into the Netscape location field. The Edit Menu features the local Find command as well. This can be used to search on a page you've already loaded from the Net to find specific text.

If you want to see what the HTML for a particular file looks like, use the Document Source command under the View menu. This will display the HTML source code that your browser uses to build a Web document. Navigator 3.0 doesn't feature standard edit commands for the View Source window, but you can highlight text blocks from here (with the mouse pointer) and use keyboard commands (Ctrl-C for copy) to move them to different documents. To save a Web document's entire HTML file, use the File menu's Save As command and choose "Source."

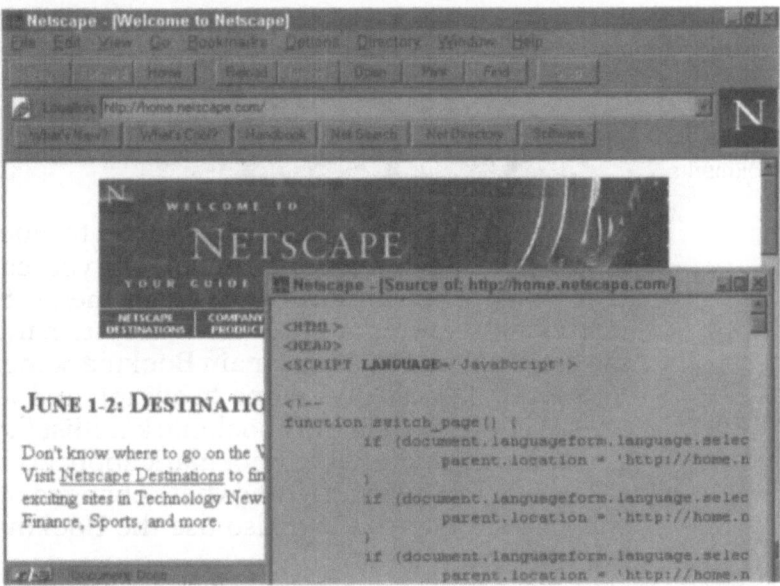

FIGURE 2.2.
HTML source in Netscape.

The View menu also features commands for reloading and refreshing pages (use these to reconnect to Web pages that may not have transferred properly or drawn correctly in your browser).

The Go menu features commands for moving between pages and accessing the default home page, and a Stop command for canceling a Web transfer. This menu also features a current history menu that lists the places you've recently visited; you can jump independently to pages on this list just by selecting them.

Navigator 3.0's enhanced Bookmark system features a pull-down menu of favorite sites, as well as a separate Bookmark application you can use to manage your bookmark collections.

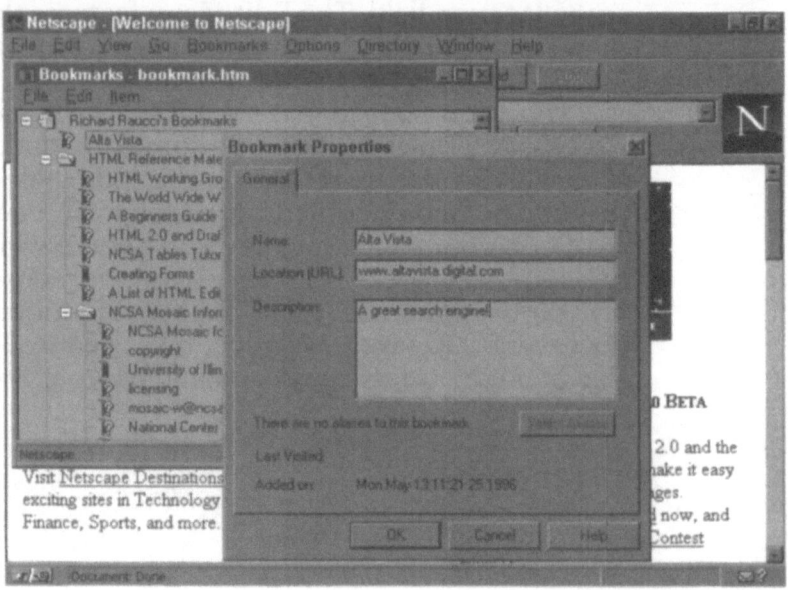

FIGURE 2.3.
Netscape
Bookmarks.

From the Bookmark menu, select Go to Bookmarks. This will launch a small Bookmark application you can use to edit and reorder bookmark links in the main menu. Some of the more interesting features of the bookmark system include the ability to make branched lists in the main Bookmark menu (to put all links to a given subject under one heading), and to insert separator lines. You can also import bookmark/hotlist files from other Web applications, and use the Bookmark application to check its own URLs over the Internet to see what's changed on the relevant Web sites. Of course, you can also use the Bookmark application to navigate the Web directly.

You can configure Netscape Navigator in a variety of ways. The main controls are located in the Options:General Preferences panel. The Appearance section lets you customize the Toolbar to show as pictures, text, or a combination of both. This section also lets you launch Netscape Mail or News automatically when you start Navigator, and to select a different home page. Use the Set Links commands to turn off automatic link underlining, and to set when your visited links will revert to the basic link color.

The Font panel lets you change the default fonts for all Web pages that Netscape loads (be very careful if you use this; it can cause many pages to format incorrectly), and also features foreign language encoding settings for viewing sites in languages

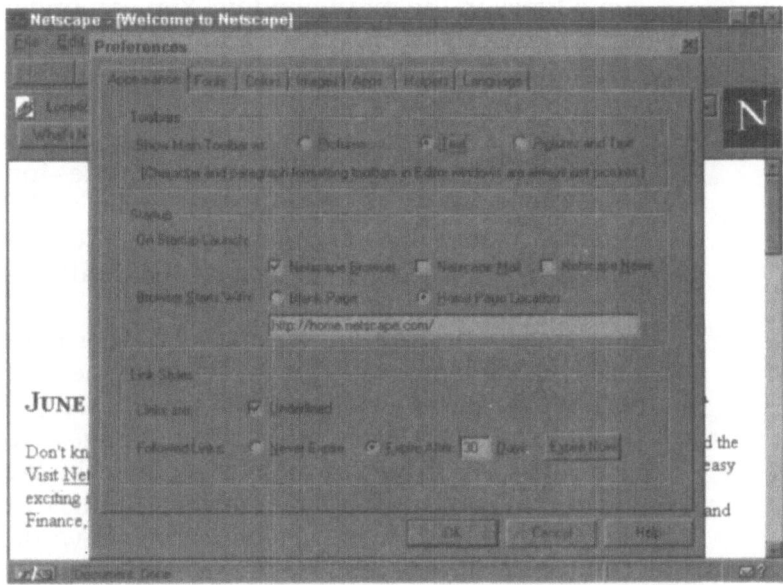

FIGURE 2.4.
Netscape
Preferences.

other than English (there's also a separate Language panel on which you can set a wide variety of foreign language types for Netscape to accept).

The Color panel, like the font settings, should be used with care. You can set alternate link and text colors and provide your own background image, but you may cause a page that has its own color and background scheme to load incorrectly. Make sure the Override Document switch is turned off if you don't want this to happen.

Under Images, you can choose a color correction scheme that will best suit your display. You may have to experiment to see which setting looks best. You can also turn off automatic image loading from here, which will significantly speed up Web page loading.

The Apps panel tells Netscape where to find certain applications you may need to reach Internet sites that don't have Web page interfaces. You can specify a path to Telnet programs from here, which will automatically launch when you need them. This panel is also where you can specify an alternate View Source editing program (like Windows Write, WordPad, or an HTML editor), which will launch instead of the internal HTML viewer.

The Helpers section lists the data types that Netscape knows about. These include in-line JPEG and GIF images, sound files, and text formats. Navigator either views these data types directly or launches external programs to handle them. In certain cases, Netscape 3.0 can use internal plug-ins to view alternate data types in the main window. You can update the Helpers section manually to change or add new data types, but this section is mainly being configured automatically when you install new helper applications.

Netscape's Mail and News features have their own panel under Options. Use this to set different font styles for Email and Usenet news messages, select mail directories and sorting styles, and specify proper mail and news servers. You also use this section to set up your Email preferences, including a link to your SIG (signature) file.

The Network preferences panel (under Options) is where you control Navigator's cache, multiple connections, and proxy servers. It's important to have a good cache setup, because Navigator uses this to store recently accessed pages from your local system (instead of getting them from over the Web). If your system has enough resources, increasing the disk and cache memory is always a good idea. Likewise, the Network Buffer Size in the Connections panel can be increased, if your system can handle it. This will increase the amount of data Netscape can move to your system at one time. You can also use the Connections panel to set the maximum number of simultaneous network connections. Navigator will use these connections to download text and image files from a Web site at the same time, or to allow you to open a separate browser window during a download to continue using the Web. The caveat is that multiple connections take a lot of bandwidth, so be careful when increasing this setting. The proxy setting needs to be configured through your system administrator, if you're connecting to the Web via a firewall. If you have a direct connection, you don't need to configure this panel.

Your Security options include the ability to disable Java and JavaScript (there have been some reports of specialized Java viruses and other Java security concerns). You can also disable security alerts that will alert you when you're submitting an insecure form or accessing a secure server. This is related to the Site Certificates panel, a list of the types of authorized servers your version of Navigator can connect to securely.

Below the menu items for Preferences under Options are the switches that will turn off the Toolbar, location panel, and/or directory buttons. You may want to turn these off if you need more viewing area in the main window (all of the functions are available through the file menu or keyboard equivalents). There's also a Java Console switch that will launch a process viewer when you download a bit of Java code. You can use this to track an applet's progress, for example. The Options menu also has an Auto Load Images switch that turns off image loading, and a

Language Encoding submenu for viewing foreign language sites.

The Directory section features links to the Netscape Web site's special areas, like the What's New and What's Cool listings of interesting Web sites, and an on-line Customer Showcase. There's also a helpful Internet directory, with links to World Wide Web search pages, and information about the Internet itself.

Under the Window menu, you can launch Netscape Mail and Netscape News. Netscape Mail is a full-featured Email system that can work with any standard network connection or dial-up Internet Access Provider. It's well integrated with Netscape (for example, URLs in Email messages will show up as navigable links, and clicking on them will launch a browser window and load the page). The News system can connect to any News server and display Newsgroup postings. You can also post News messages from here. A good feature of Netscape's News reader is that it can automatically decode picture files and display them in the main window.

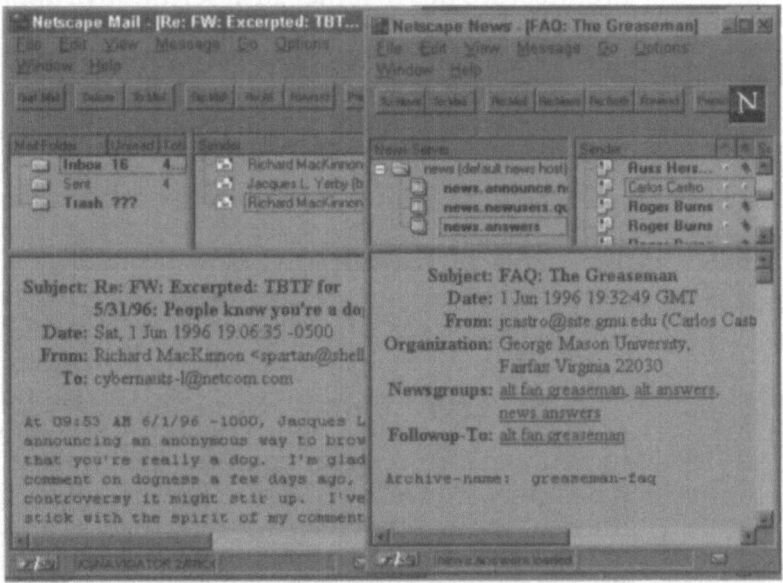

FIGURE 2.5.
Netscape Mail and News.

Netscape's plug-in architecture is one of its most advanced features. Plug-ins can add functionality to Navigator without having to run as external programs. These can be used to view documents in alternative formats (like Adobe Acrobat files), run sophisticated animations (via Shockwave), or play live audio (via RealAudio). Netscape currently ships a PowerPack of plug-ins for Windows; version 2.0 includes viewers for Word documents, VRML (Virtual Reality Markup Language) virtual reality browsers, and players for Shockwave animation and audio. Find out more at `http://home.netscape.com/comprod/power_pack_summary.html`. Netscape also has information on plug-ins you can download yourself at `http://home.netscape.com/comprod/mirror/navcomponents_download.html`, in areas for 3D and animation viewers, audio and video players, business utilities, and presentation software.

Netscape 3.0 also includes supplemental special features that can significantly enhance your Web experience. The Live3D software is a VRML virtual reality browser that works as a plug-in. There's also LiveVideo support, which allows you to play AVI movies inside a Web page, and LiveAudio, for listening to embedded audio. CoolTalk is an Internet phone application that can let you have conversations over the Net, complete with a chat window (for typing text) and a shared whiteboard (for sharing files). Navigator 3.0 continues to support the Java programming language, with enhanced support for JavaScript. The LiveConnect architecture ties together JavaScript, Java applets, and Navigator plug-ins with a direct communication subsystem, for increased performance. The Netscape Administration Kit (for customizing and locking user preferences) and enhanced SSL (Secure Socket Layer) security round out the large list of new features in Netscape 3.0.

Microsoft Internet Explorer 3.0

Internet Explorer 3.0 works with NT 4.0 and above. It's a standard variant of Spyglass Mosaic, and provides Web browsing capabilities a little below Netscape 3.0 (no support for plug-ins, for example). The main features include a sizable viewing window, a toolbar with buttons for common program functions, a location panel (that shows the URL you're currently visiting), and a status line (for indicating Web transfer progress and link locations).

The File menu has functions for opening Web URLs and local files. You can also send Email from here, and access print commands (although there's no print preview). Use the History panel to get a list of recently visited sites that you can jump between by clicking on them (there's also a drop-down history menu in the location panel). The Edit menu has standard Cut, Copy, and Paste commands (useful for selecting text in a Web document or for transferring a URL to the location panel). This menu also features the local Find panel, which you can use to search for text in a Web document that you've already loaded.

The View menu is where you can customize the main window

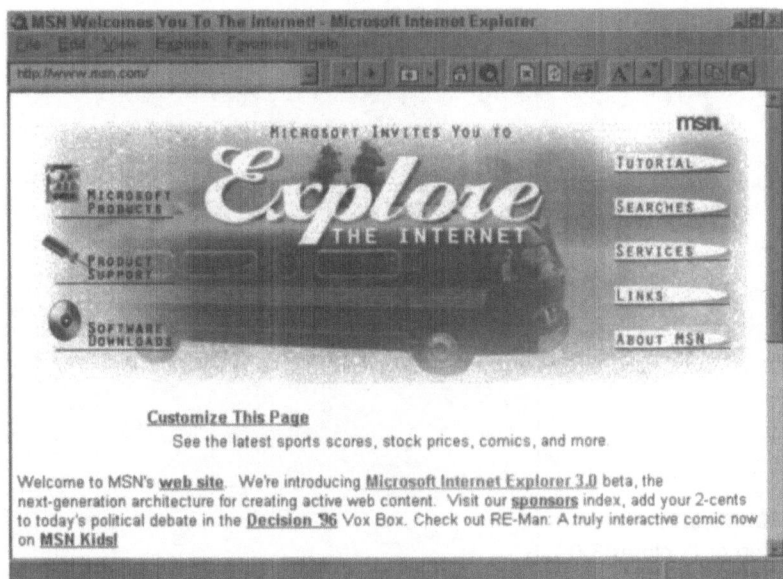

FIGURE 2.6.
MS Internet Explorer
3.0 main window.

fully. You can turn off the Toolbar, location panel, and status bar to gain more viewing room. You can also change the font sizes in Web pages from here, and set the text styles to plain, fancy, or mixed. To speed up Web transfers if you have a slow connection, you can turn off images from here. Use the Source command to view the HTML code in a particular document (the default viewer is Notepad, but you can change this).

The View:Options panel features settings for Web page appearance (pictures, sound, animation control, font selection, and link/text color), file type registration (where you register helper applications), and security (including an Internet security tutorial, and programmable system alerts). You can also change the default home page, and set a preferred Internet search site that you can connect to via the Toolbar. Use the Advanced settings panel to change cache and history file settings.

The Go menu has the same functions for moving between pages as the Toolbar, and commands for loading the start and search pages. The Favorites menu keeps a drop-down list of favorite Web site locations, and you can also launch a panel that lets you edit and import Favorites files (also known as hotlists and bookmarks). Help is available for Internet Explorer under the File:Help menu, and you can also find a search panel just for IE help here.

Advanced features in MS Internet Explorer 3.0 include a News panel that will allow you to configure Internet Explorer as a Usenet News reader, so you can connect to newsgroups directly,

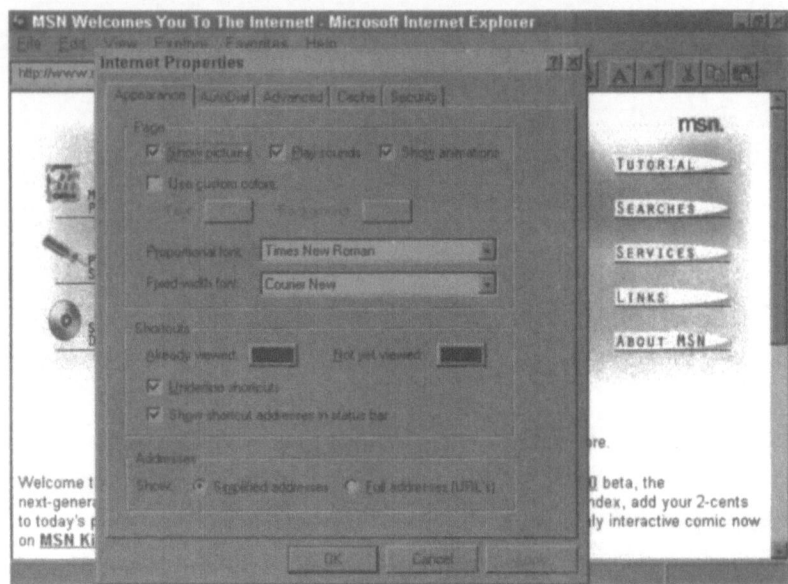

FIGURE 2.7.
Internet Explorer 3.0
Options panel.

and a standard Internet Email reader. The included NetMeeting software lets you make telephone calls directly over the Net. There's also support for Real Audio, an enhanced audio file format, and a virtual reality VRML browser add-in. Multimedia technologies via ActiveX are also included, which provide support for direct animation, video, and audio support in Web pages, as well as custom-embedded control systems and Java support. MS IE 3.0 also comes with an Administration Kit for customizing and locking browser preferences.

NCSA Mosaic 2.1

NCSA Mosaic is the grandfather of all Web browsers, and it still has many interesting, unique features. Version 2.1 for NT includes internal support for standard data types (.JPG and .GIF files, and .AU .AIFF audio) as well as for .BMP images and .WAV audio files. There are also AutoSurfing capabilities (a way for Mosaic to move between links on a page automatically), and Internet collaboration features.

The main window features the requisite menu system and Toolbar, as well as a location panel, set above the main viewing window. There's also a three-part status panel at the bottom of the screen, with a built-in clock, and icon views of Web data types as they download.

Under the File menu, there are standard commands for open-

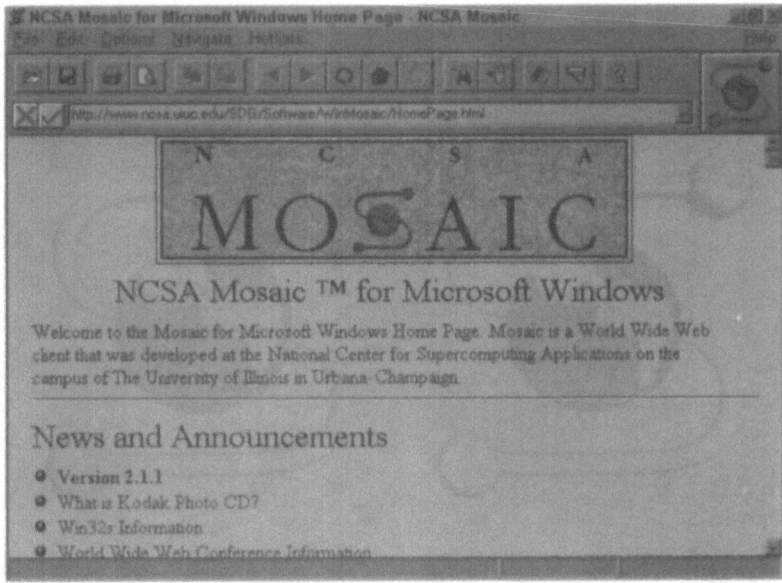

FIGURE 2.8.
Mosaic 2.1 main
window.

ing URLs and local documents. You can also save Web documents from here, in HTML format or as text. The print commands include a preview window and page setup features. If you're properly set up (in the View:Options:News panel), you can launch Mosaic's internal Newsgroup reader from the File menu. There's also a good external Emailer built-in, and a Document Source viewer that will let you view HTML files.

Use the File:Collaborate command to open an interactive collaboration session window. You can host or join a session via IP addresses, and use a text window to pass messages like a common Chat program. You can also link multiple sessions by distributing the current host's URL (and following link URLs) to every participant's main viewer window at the same time.

The Edit menu lets you copy and paste text, but there's no cut command (use Ctrl-X if you need this). There's also a local Find command for searching on a particular page.

Under Options, you can turn off the toolbar, location panel, and status line to gain more viewing area. You can also maximize the viewing area by switching into Presentation mode from here. This will turn off everything except the main viewing field (use Alt-P to restore the program to the default settings). The Options menu also features Mosaic's comprehensive Preferences panels, with settings for Anchor styles (change link colors and updating patterns) and Audio features (set .WAV files to play with common Mosaic features, like opening a Web document). There's also a superior Cache control panel, with an Advanced Disk Cache Man-

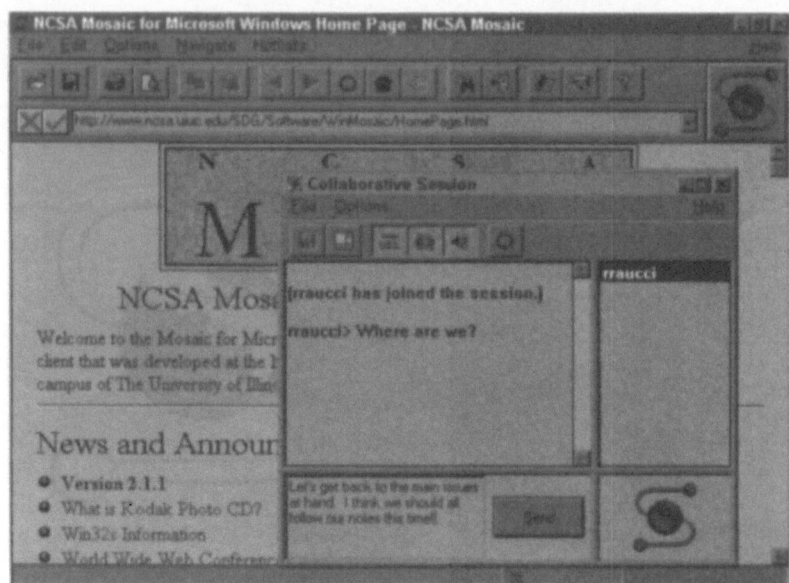

FIGURE 2.9.
Mosaic
Collaboration
window.

ager that gives you a large degree of control over the way Mosaic handles files. The Directories panel lets you change the default downloading directory, and set when Mosaic's global history and News configuration files will be stored.

Use the Options:Preferences:Document panel to set the background color and in-line image styles for Web pages that you view. You can also set an alternate home page here, and turn off automatic image and display loading. The Fonts section lets you change the default font settings for all HTML tags in a Web document (this is not an advised course of action, as it can scramble many Web pages).

The Preferences:News panel is where you'll enter the address of your Network News server. You can also change the way Newsgroups will sort inside your browser. The Printing panel allows you a good range of control over how you print a Web document, including the options to include the document title and location on each page, and to add the date and time. For NT users behind a firewall on a corporate LAN, use the Proxy panel to set up servers for Internet access. The Preferences:Services panel lets you configure Email, FTP, telnet, and TCP/IP chat settings, as well as a network timeout limit.

You may have to configure the Preferences:Tables settings in Mosaic to let pages created with Netscape's table formatting appear properly. Use the Viewers panel to add or change Helper applications, and the Window panel to customize how the program will look and where it will show up on your desktop.

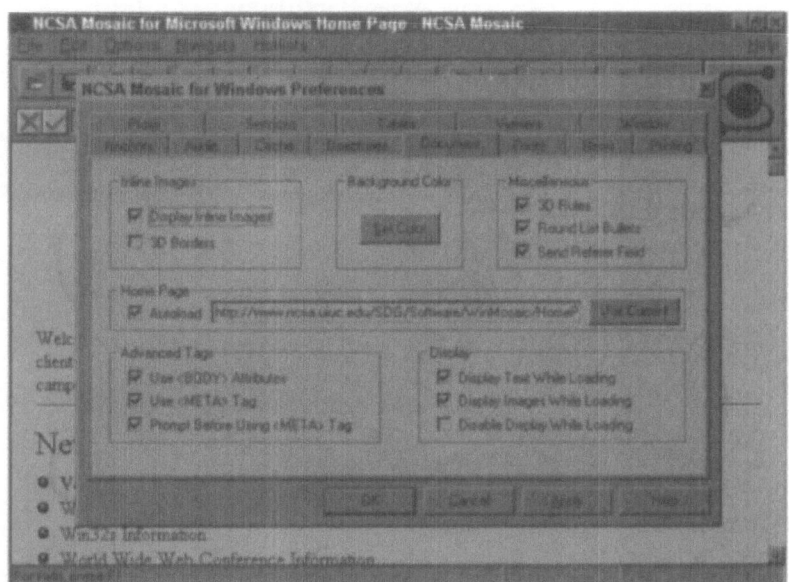

FIGURE 2.10.
Mosaic Preferences.

The Navigate menu has commands for moving between Web pages and for displaying Mosaic's session history list of recently viewed documents. You can also launch the Advanced Hotlist Manager from here. The Hotlist manager can import hotlist and bookmark files, and will automatically alphabetize its own list and remove links that are no longer valid. You can also generate a hotlist from the links on a page (very useful), and use the AutoSurf command to link serially to the links in the bookmark window.

The AutoSurf feature lets you automatically connect to each link on a page, to the links on those pages as well, and so on. This will let you surf the Web without having to touch your computer, and each page visited will be saved in your cache. You can then view the Web pages while off-line.

Oracle PowerBrowser

Oracle PowerBrowser is a specially designed Web browser that works with standard Web documents as well as with Oracle's Network Loadable Objects and Oracle Basic programs. There's also built-in support for ODBC database connectivity. Version 1.5 also supports Java applets and RSA security, like Netscape 2.0.

The main Browser window features a standard menu system and a Toolbar for accessing common program features. There's also a location panel, with buttons for connecting to a URL and

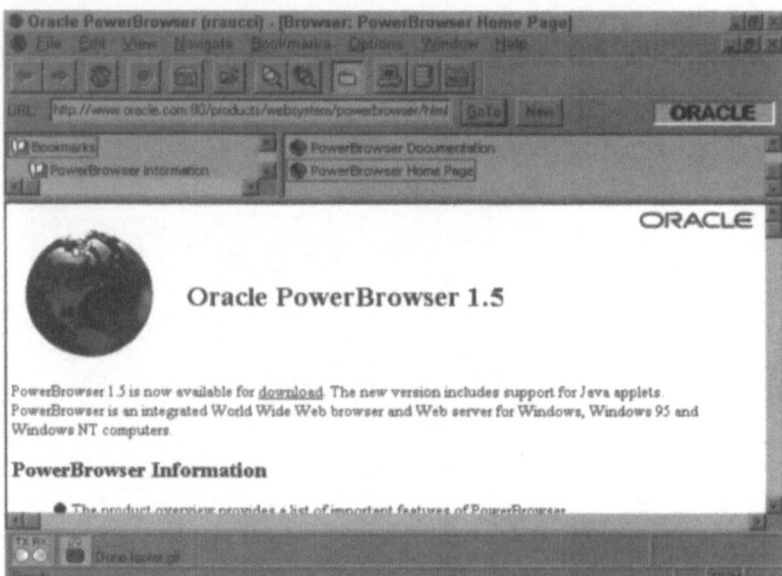

FIGURE 2.11.
PowerBrowser main window.

for launching a new browser window. PowerBrowser's main viewing window is divided into an integrated bookmark/history list located on the left side and a Web browser view on the right. You can go directly to any link in your bookmarks by clicking on it. The bottom status line features a security icon, a data transfer display, and link location information.

There's also a Server window view; this is used to implement PowerBrowser as a personal Web server, and it includes a home page creation wizard, an HTML editor, and a setup for implementing ODBC queries from your server. It's fairly easy to get connected as a server from here, and you should be careful with this panel.

The NLO view lets you interact with Network Loadable Objects, Oracle's version of embedded controls for Web documents (like Microsoft's Active X). There are also some preloaded objects you can view while off-line.

The PowerBrowser main menu has standard commands for loading URLs and local files and for saving them to disk. There's also a Send mail command that will open a small Email panel, and Print functions.

The Edit menu has only a Copy command (no cut or paste), and Local and Net Find commands (the former will search the text in a page that is currently loaded; the latter will connect to the Internet search engine that you specify).

Use the View menu to turn off the Toolbar, Location line, and Frame/browser status bars (to gain more viewing area). You can

FIGURE 2.12.
Personal Server
page.

hide the Bookmark/History panes (for a more conventional Web browser view), and reorient them to horizontal or vertical alignment. This menu also allows you to copy the Web page text directly to the clipboard, and to view/edit the HTML source in a document.

The Navigate Menu features standard back and forth commands, and you can also jump up a folder level in bookmarks from here. There are also commands for reloading pages, stopping file transfers, and clearing the main page.

The Options:Preferences panel lets you set preferences for proxy servers, disk and memory cache, user controls, and security parameters. You can also configure network timeouts from here, and add helper applications to the system.

Tango!

The Tango Web browser, from ALIS, is a version of Spyglass Mosaic that is designed specifically for international businesses. You can set the menus and control panels to any of six languages instantly (German, French, English, Italian, Spanish, and Russian), and there are a number of language preference settings and character sets you can specify (for use with Web pages that support them, of course).

FIGURE 2.13.
The ALIS Tango Web
site.

The main window features a standard menu system, with an integrated Web command Toolbar. Directly below that is the location panel, with a pair of Web page browsing buttons to the left. Underneath the main viewing window is a common status/transfer progress bar.

Under the File Menu there are commands for launching a new browser window and for loading in a URL or a local file. There are also common print and page setup commands (but no print previewing), and you can also save a Web document as text or HTML format.

The Edit Menu features standard cut, copy, and paste commands, as well as a local find panel. This menu also features a View Source command that will show the loaded document's HTML source in a new browser window. Use the Edit:Security submenu to configure modules from First Virtual, RSA (Digest Authentication), and CERN (Basic Authentication). The Edit: Preferences panels let you configure Tango in a variety of ways. Use the Display settings to change how a page loads and displays, or to turn off automatic image loading. The Fonts panel lets you change the font sizes and types in your Web documents, and the Color settings are for the default backgrounds and link color schemes (use both of these with care, as most Web pages are designed with their own schemes in mind). The Cache setting is straightforward (increase the cache level, if you have the system resources, to improve performance), and the Proxy server settings need to be used only if you're configuring Tango from behind a firewall. The Miscellaneous settings include switches to turn off the Toolbar and location panel (to gain more viewing area), and places to specify Email and NetNews configuration information. Finally, use the Edit:Helpers panel to set up Tango with alternate image, text, video, or audio helper applications.

The Navigate Menu has standard items for moving between Web pages, and a set of links to interesting pages on the ALIS Web site. You can also reach the History window from here (for a list of recently viewed sites), and launch an integrated Hotlist list that will show up on the left side of the main window (somewhat like Oracle's PowerBrowser).

As mentioned before, Tango supports multiple languages from the Language Menu. You can change the User Interface to a different language, edit your language preferences, and add character-set definitions to your browser.

The main Tango Help system is in the form of HTML files that load directly into your browser from the local system. You can also connect to the ALIS site for up-to-date information.

Getting Connected

Now that you have your preferred Web browser under consideration, you'll want to get your Net connection under way.

If you're on a corporate LAN with access to the Internet, your system administrator should be able to configure NT's built-in TCP/IP networking protocols to get your connection to the Net working properly. Otherwise, you can connect to an Internet Service Provider (which may be a part of your corporate LAN or a third-party vendor like PSI or EarthLink) via MS Remote Access and a fast modem. You may also want to consider ISDN (Integrated Services Digital Network) equipment for a faster connection, which makes Web browsing much easier.

Although the standard phone line system is all you really need to run a Web browser, you'll find that it has built-in limitations that will affect the kind of performance you'll get. The standard POTS (Plain Old Telephone System) is still derived from analog technology, and geared for voice transmission. This means that the computer's digital information has to be converted to analog in order to transfer down the POTS line. That's what a standard modem does: it modulates digital computer signals into analog to send them out and demodulates them back into digital as they come in. An analog signal can be considered as an erratic wave formation. The information it transmits is passing over older circuits that were designed in the 1940s for voice, and the translated data has to make the analog journey back and forth in this inefficient format, not to mention the overhead involved in the translation process.

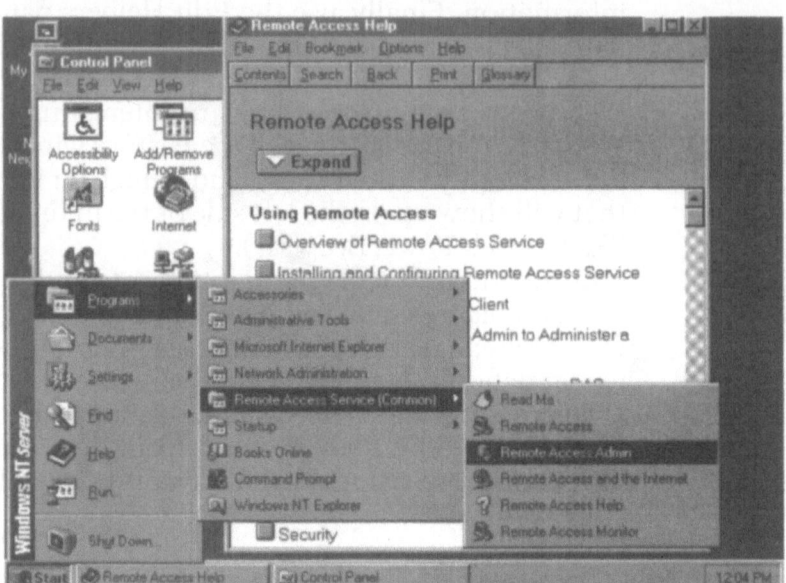

FIGURE 2.14.
MS Remote Access Help file.

ISDN, on the other hand, uses a digital format from end to end. This means you don't need a modem; ISDN uses what's called a DSU (Data Service Unit) to move digital computer data over digital lines from end to end. This is more like a square wave, with no erratic acoustic patterning found in an analog signal. With more precise digital control over the data involved, a sustained high-speed connection can be made. NT 3.5 and up is already ISDN-compatible; you won't need extra software to use it.

ISDN is becoming more and more available in residential versions, and requires little extra equipment. Microsoft supports ISDN via its ISDN home page, `http://www.microsoft.com/windows/getisdn/`.

The only other equipment you'll need with this board is an NT1 adapter. This is a Network Termination unit; it connects your ISDN equipment to the ISDN equipment at your Internet access provider's site. It sits between your PC's ISDN equipment and your ISDN phone jack. It's becoming more common for ISDN adapters to include Network Termination built into the base unit, and we expect the separate terminators to be phased out in the near future.

Once you have the hardware installed and the access provider selected (make sure they are ISDN-capable), you have to have your ISDN line installed. Contact your local phone service to find out if ISDN is available in your area. Use the ISDN profiles provided by your Internet access provider to tell your phone company how to set up your line. In this case we used the profiles

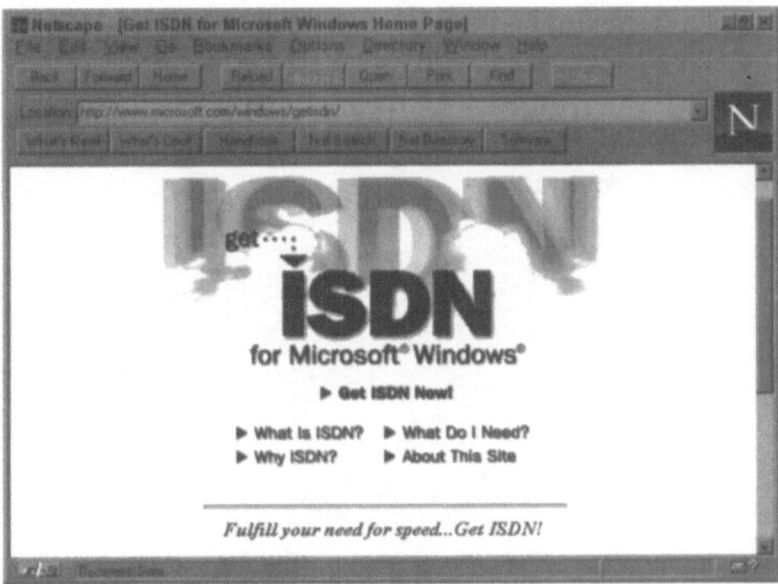

FIGURE 2.15.
MS ISDN Page.

provided by PSI to order our ISDN line. The line can be installed either to a new phone jack or in the place of an existing line.

Costs for our example line (San Francisco area, Pacific Bell) ran to $75 for the installation labor, $35 to switch the line from a standard analog line to a digital line, and $15 for the first monthly fee. For $125 we had a digital ISDN line that more closely approximated the high-speed networks that Mosaic was designed to be used with. A caveat: an ISDN line is not a standard phone line; if you change an old line over, you can't use standard modems, phones, or FAX equipment with it any longer (you can even possibly *damage* a standard phone by connecting it to an ISDN jack). Special ISDN telecommunications equipment is available, but it's certainly not as common as analog equipment.

Once you have the ISDN line in, you can use the Microsoft ISDN connection software to set up your system. Enter your ISDN information, including your ISDN SPID (Service Profile ID) numbers provided by the phone company. You also set up your direct dial number to your access provider, and your account information (user name and password) if you need to use authentication.

Another type of ISDN adapter is one that connects to a serial port, like a modem. PSI certifies the Motorola BitSURFR as a personal ISDN adapter. It includes an NT1 adapter, so you don't have to pay for additional hardware. It only runs on ISDN lines, and is somewhat limited in its connectivity to asynchronous PPP (analog modem style). While faster data communications are achieved with this unit over standard modems, it uses the same type of data link as a standard modem, so it's not as fast as internal ISDN cards. Its primary advantages are its relatively low cost and the fact that you can move it between different systems and sites easily (for example, between home and office ISDN accounts).

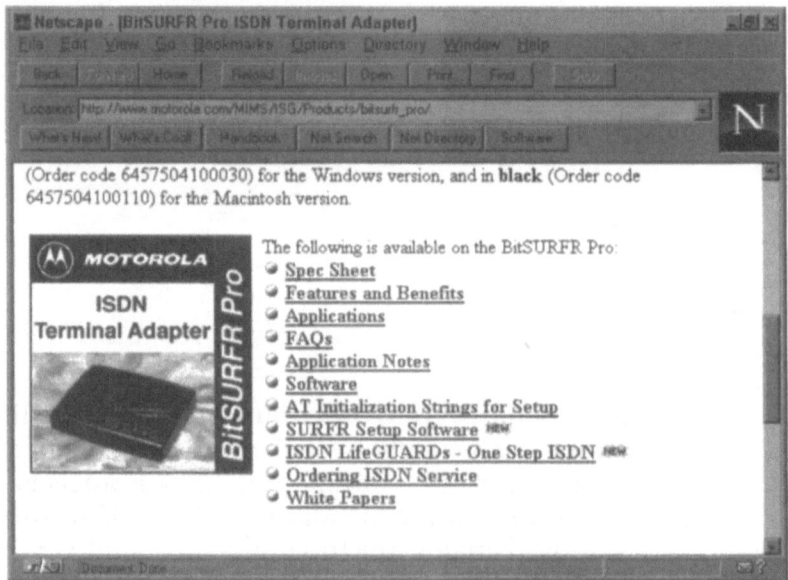

FIGURE 2.16.
The BitSURFR home page at Motorola's Web site.

You might want to consider an external ISDN unit that includes a modem, like Motorola's HTMA 200. This unit combines an ISDN terminal adapter with an integrated NT1 unit and a fast V32 14.4/28.8K modem. It not only works as an ISDN adapter (using a standard PC serial port, and subject to the same current limitations to asynchronous PPP as other external ISDN adapters), it also functions as an analog modem over your ISDN line. This means that you can connect to your Internet account via ISDN, and to an on-line service via the modem function. The HTMA 200 includes Windows configuration software.

3Com also has a hybrid modem and ISDN adapter, called the Impact (formerly the QuickAccess Remote). This works in the same manner as the HTMA 200, and also includes high-speed modem emulation. 3Com also provides Windows configuration software for this unit. You can use this software to upgrade the unit's firmware and software configurations, and there are also instructions on how to connect your PC to the Net via PPP with the Impact.

The hybrid modem is a good solution to the problem of can-

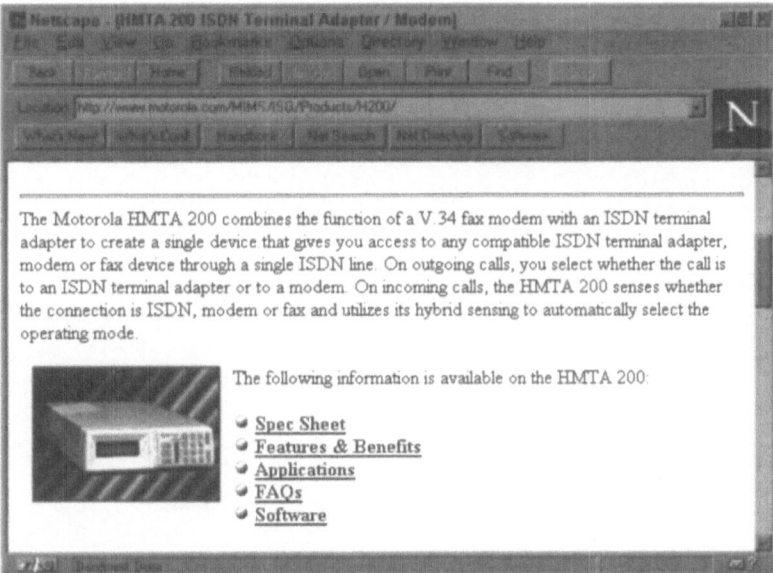

FIGURE 2.17.
Motorola's HMTA
200 (from the Web
site).

celing an existing analog line by making it into a digital ISDN line. This unit gives you back the modem functionality thereby lost.

It's especially interesting to note how the ISDN service provider, your Internet access provider, the ISDN hardware, and your Internet software all interrelate. In this case, the ISDN service provider brought the line to the PC, configuring the line to match the ISDN adapter card or external unit. The ISDN equipment was certified by PSI (the Internet Access Provider) as being compatible with their Internet service, and was listed as being compatible with their Internet connectivity software. It's important to have this same chain working for whatever Windows NT ISDN Internet equipment you choose.

3
Web Servers for Windows NT

If you decide to run a Web server, you should carefully consider what you want to serve before you choose software. The main issues are Web content creation and interactive content capability, scalability and traffic handling, security, and ease of use. If you want to set up a Web page to promote a company, for example, will your Web server software came with graphics and HTML software that will help you make your pages? If you plan to add interactive content, what kind of scripting does your server software support (like CGI, Perl, and/or Java)? What level of demand do you expect your site to have per day, and how does the Web server software scale up to large numbers of connections?

Some other important features to look for in an NT Web server are the ability of the program to run as a system service (this allows better integration with NT subsystems), a good graphical setup and maintenance interface, and remote administration capabilities. You'll also want performance analysis tools (either as generated reports or as real-time Web site activity monitoring) and user logs. Most Web servers support CGI scripting for interactive Web applications (like forms), and programming languages like Perl or Java are a good inclusion (with Visual Basic becoming more important in the NT Web world). You'll also want to look for features like image map support and server side includes, Web programming features that can add value to your Web sites.

Security is a real concern over the Internet, and most NT Web servers support basic Unix-style authentication (username/password directory authentication), with SSL (Secure Sockets Layer), Secure HTTP (S-HTTP), and RSA Public Key Encryption being offered in some packages as stronger security measures.

You may also want to look for Web servers with support for other protocols besides HTTP, like direct FTP, Gopher, Usenet News, and SMTP Email server capability. Some Web server packages also include Web search engines and integrated database support.

NT Web Servers on Multiple Platforms

These Web server programs are available for high-performance RISC processor systems, as well as for standard Intel-based computers.

Commercial Products

Netscape's Web server products (`http://home.netscape.com/comprod/server_central/`) include a full range of NT-capable products. The SuiteSpot line includes LiveWire Pro (discussed below) and your choice of a server product; the Enterprise server is the best choice for maintaining a Web site. Netscape also offers a FastTrack server designed specifically for the Web.

The Enterprise and Fast Track server lines both include graphical installation routines (which will also upgrade earlier Netscape Communications and Commerce server products). Their management software is a JavaScript-based GUI (Graphical User Interface) that features online security monitoring, performance tuning, and remote management via secure Web clients. There's also SMTP Email support, basic RDMS database connectivity, and an integrated full-text search engine. Java is a large part of Netscape's server line, with Java and JavaScript support built directly into their servers. There's also support for CGI, Perl, and WinCGI via Visual Basic. Web content creation is available in Netscape Web servers via Navigator Gold, an HTML document creator directly integrated into the Navigator browser. Netscape's servers support SSL 3.0 security.

The optional LiveWire Pro (an add-on to the Fast Track and Enterprise servers) features a suite of tools that includes a graphical Site Manager, an external link checking program (to verify hypertext links in a Web document), and HTML Wizards and templates for many different types of Web pages. LiveWire Pro also includes image and document file conversion utilities (useful for creating Web content from different sources), a JavaScript compiler (for creating applications that include Java, HTML, and images) and native support for Informix, Oracle, Sybase, Illustra, and ODBC object databases (including a developer version of Informix with an unlimited run-time license). Software is available for Intel, MIPS, and Alpha NT hardware.

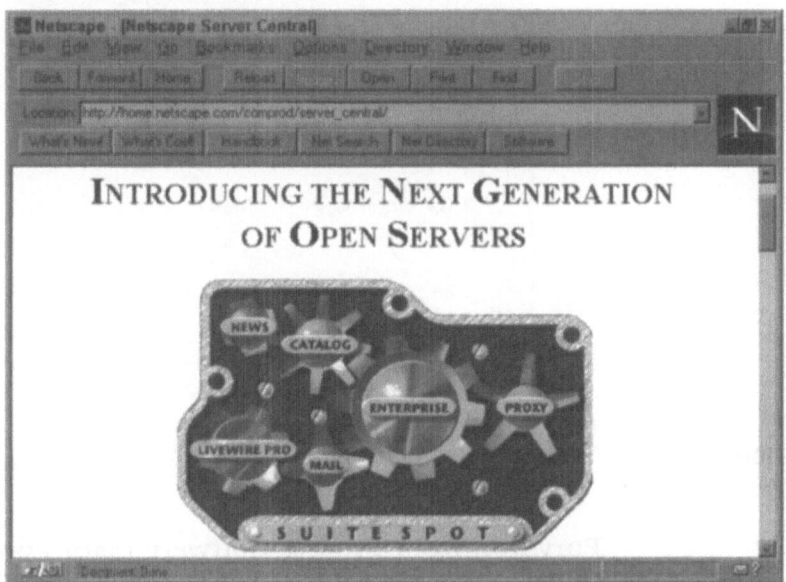

FIGURE 3.1.
Netscape Server Central.

Microsoft's Internet Information Server (MS IIS) (http://www.microsoft.com/Infoserv/) is especially well integrated into the NT operating system, but it lacks some of the more advanced features of Netscape's server line. MS IIS includes a good GUI setup and maintenance program (the Internet Service Manager) that works remotely, and account management via the NT Server administration tools. Performance tracking is via the NT Performance Monitor, and SSL security is standard. There's a good level of integration with MS BackOffice as well, and some third-party Internet-aware applications for BackOffice are being developed. Logging to an ODBC database or to a flat text file is supported. Standard Web programming via CGI/Perl is included, as well as via ISAPI (the Internet Server Applications Programming Interface), a programming extension into the Windows NT API that uses Dynamic Link Libraries and supports Win32 application development for the Internet.

The Internet Information Server also includes Gopher and FTP server software, and database support via the Internet Database

Connector (for SQL and Open Database databases). Client software for Win 3.1, Win 95, and NT is included (Microsoft's Internet Explorer), and IIS is available for Intel, MIPS, Alpha, and PowerPC NT systems.

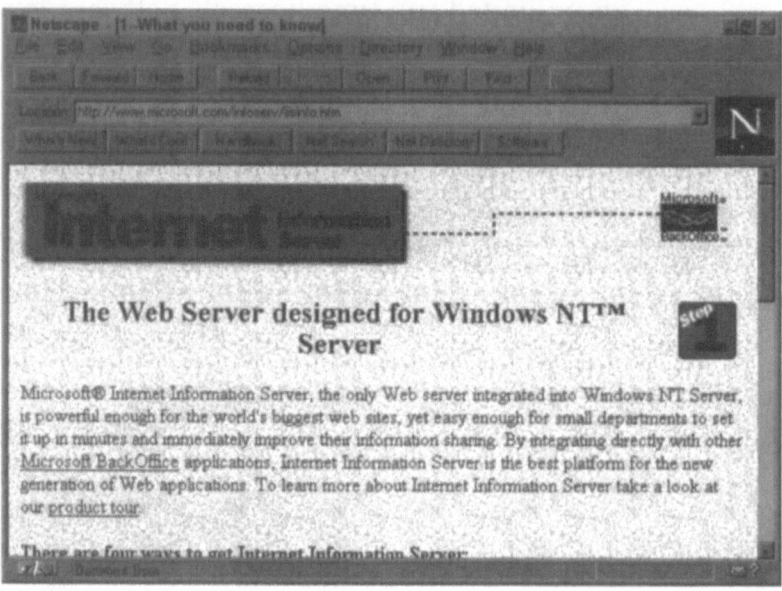

FIGURE 3.2.
MS IIS.

Purveyor, from Process Software (http://www.process.com), is also well integrated into the NT system. It provides good setup/maintenance software, with custom performance report generation via NT's Performance Monitor, and a Log Viewer application (for storing and generating usage log reports). Security is via Basic Authentication (in version 1.2), and is also maintained via NT's File Manager user controls. Process co-developed ISAPI with Microsoft, and uses it to connect Purveyor with Process's full-text search engine (Verity Topic) for fast access. Purveyor also includes a Data Wizard for ODBC connectivity to SQL and other database formats.

Standard CGI programming and ISAPI is supported, and Purveyor also includes HTML templates for use in creating home pages, as well as sample HTML-CGI applications that can be customized and adapted for specific business uses. Purveyor also comes with a CD-ROM called "Cool Tools," a set of freeware and shareware HTML authoring and conversion programs, mail and gopher server software, and WWW development tools. It's available for Intel and Alpha NT systems.

GNNserver (http://www.tools.gnn.com/), from America Online's GNN company, features HTML forms-based Web server setup

FIGURE 3.3.
Purveyor.

and administration, a complete HTML authoring suite, good database connectivity, and SSL security. The authoring suite is GNNpress, a WYSIWYG (what you see is what you get) Web editor integrated into GNNserver, with HTML editing, image map controls, and Web site administration built in. GNNserver also features a full-text search engine that can also generate page hyperlink suggestions, and a complete implementation of the Illustra DBMS (with support for other databases via ODBC and nsdb database protocols, the GNNserver Database Services module).

TCL scripting is supported, for building interactive Web applications without having to use CGI. You can also update the TCL scripts via an HTML forms interface. There's also a complete C API, for programming more complex Web routines, database drivers, logging functions, and TCL scripts. GNNserver is available for Intel and Alpha NT hardware.

Internet Factory's Commerce Builder (`http://www.aristosoft.com/ifact/inet.htm`) is custom configured as an on-line store. The On-line Catalog Builder interviews you as to your product descriptions, prices, and tax information, then builds an interactive Web shopping application. The Commerce Builder Web server software comes with SSL and RSA Public Key Encryption for secure transactions. The GUI setup and maintenance software can be used remotely. CGI scripting and image map handling is supported.

Commerce Builder also includes a ChatRoom system, for live simultaneous chat via a Web browser. You can set up different

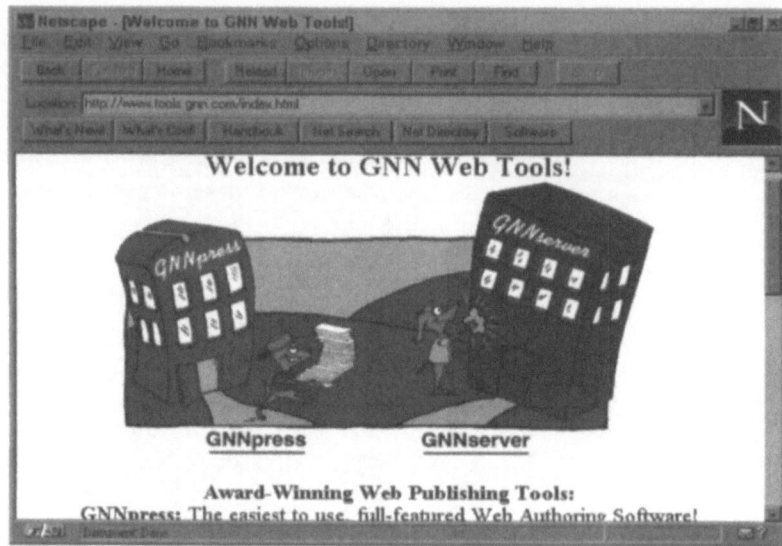

FIGURE 3.4.
GNNserver.

chat rooms for your on-line users to add value to your Web sites. The Web server software is available for Intel, Alpha, and Pow-erPC NT systems.

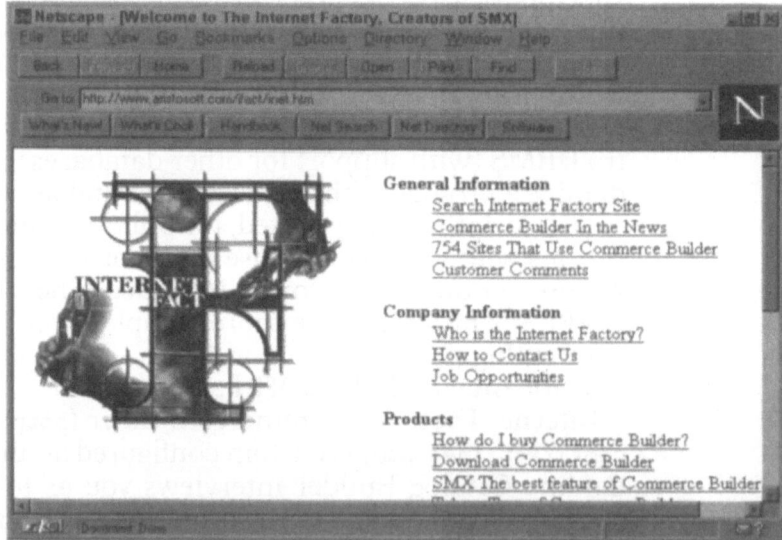

FIGURE 3.5.
Commerce Builder.

Freeware/Shareware

EMWAC (http://emwac.ed.ac.uk/html/internet_toolchest/https/ contents.htm) is a free NT Web server developed by the Edinburgh University's European Microsoft Windows NT Academic Centre (EMWAC). It includes a GUI Web site maintenance program and custom logging via the NT Event Manager. The search engine included is the WAIS Toolkit for Windows NT. EMWAC software can be downloaded for Intel, MIPS, Alpha, and PowerPC NT systems.

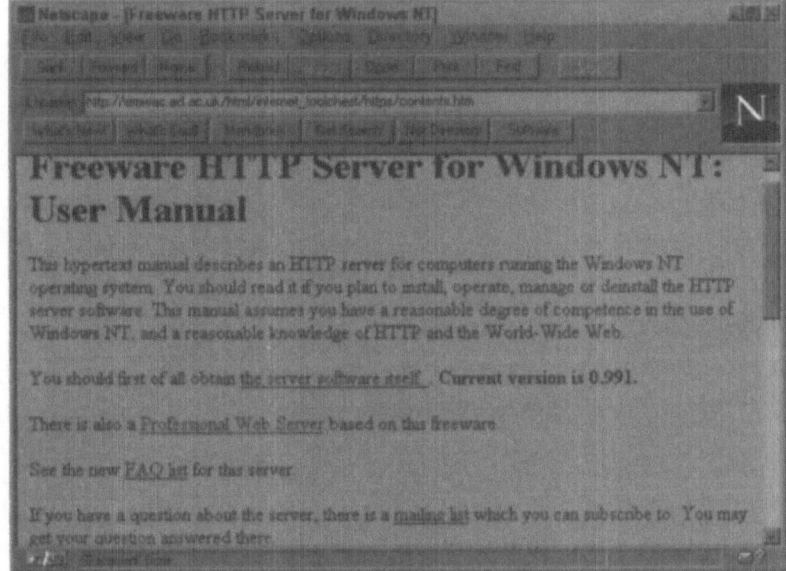

FIGURE 3.6.
EMWAC.

NT Web Servers for Intel-Based Systems

These Web servers were designed with the ubiquitous Intel 486-Pentium-PentiumPro platform in mind, but you should check with the vendors to see if there are ports to other platforms.

Commercial Products

The Internet Connection server (http://www.ics.raleigh.ibm. com/) is IBM's entry into the Web server market. The 4.1 release supports a custom IBM HTTP API for writing extensions to server-side routines (such as generating custom Web pages and system alerts). There's also standard CGI support and server-side includes. Internet Connection features customized log formats (for error and user access tracking), and SSL security.

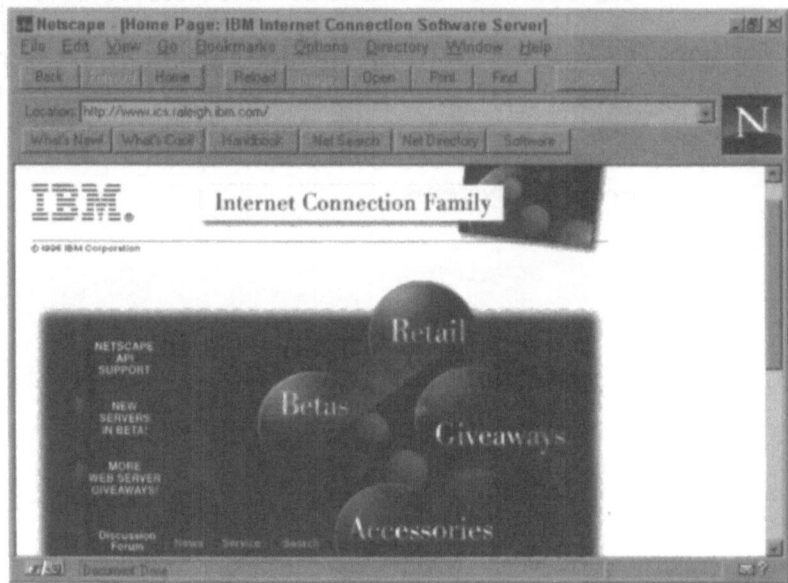

Alibaba (`http://alibaba.austria.eu.net/DOCS/`) is a full-featured NT Web server package. It includes AliAuth, an access control and document administration tool, and AliAdmin, for Web server administration. Optional SSL security is available, and CGI scripting is standard (with ISAPI and DLL support). Built-in Server Side Includes with custom extensions (like page counters) are also included. There's also support for extended access and error log file formats.

CyberPresence Secure SSL Internet Server (`http://www.cyberpi.com/`) features SSL encryption security, an integrated full text search engine, and a graphical traffic pattern analyzer tool. There is also support for a variety of log file types. CyberPresence supports CGI via standard Perl, ISAPI, and their own FastCGI subsystem, a Visual C++ DLL-based CGI toolset that includes preprogrammed modules you can use in your own Web applications. HTML support includes integrated image-map control and layout wizards for domain creation and simple home page building.

FTP Software's Esplanade Web server (`http://www.ftp.com/esplanade`) includes a wide range of document conversion tools. These built-in converters can automatically serve documents and images in non-HTML/MIME formats to Web browsers. Esplanade also features graphical setup and management software like Web Reporter, a customizable graphical activity analysis tool that

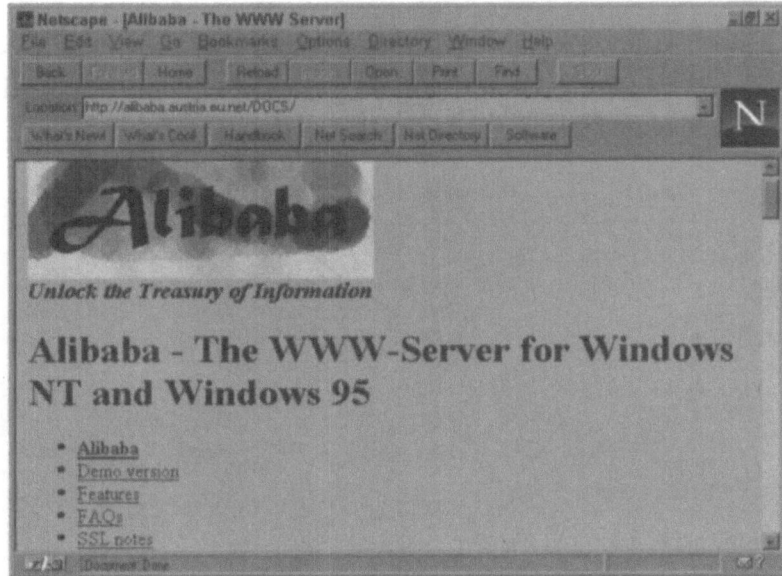

FIGURE 3.8.
Alibaba.

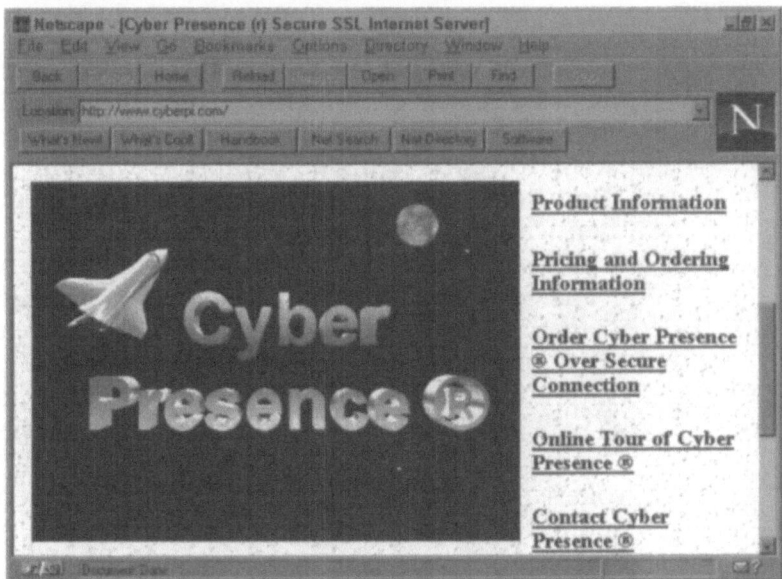

FIGURE 3.9.
CyberPresence.

works with NT log files. Database connectivity is via an ODBC Database Connectivity tool, a graphical design manager for creating HTML queries to SQL databases. SSL security is standard, and Esplanade ships with a SSL-enabled 32-bit Enhanced Mosaic browser (for verifying Web server operation). HTML interactivity via CGI Perl is also supported.

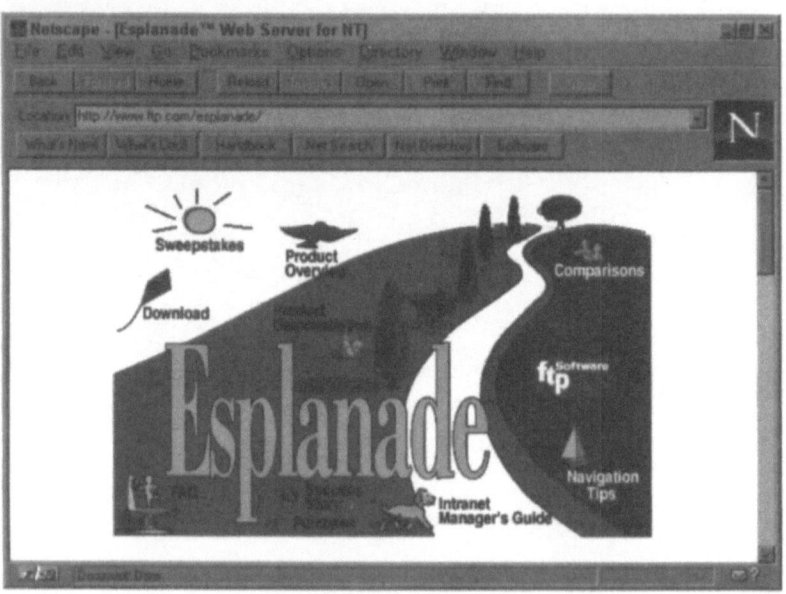

FIGURE 3.10.
Esplanade.

The FolkWeb NT Web server (http://www.ilar.com/folkweb.htm) has a standard set of features, including a FolkWeb NT Control Panel (for administrating server settings), and database connectivity (for connecting to databases without using CGI scripts). There's also support for access and error logging, and Basic Authentication (username/password). HTML features include CGI Perl support and interactive image-map controls.

The SAIC-HTTP Web server (http://wwwserver.itl.saic.com/) is an SSL-secure server package that also features security via NT's User Manager. The software includes a graphical administration tool (with remote admin capability via Remote Access), as well as HTML handling features like image-map control and CGI scripting. SAIC-HTTP's Style Sheets are templates that invoke server-side include functions for documents that match predefined criteria, meaning you can control server includes more efficiently.

Spry's SafetyWeb (http://server.spry.com) includes SSL security, ODBC database support, and Architext Software's Excite Web search engine. Local and remote setup and control is avail-

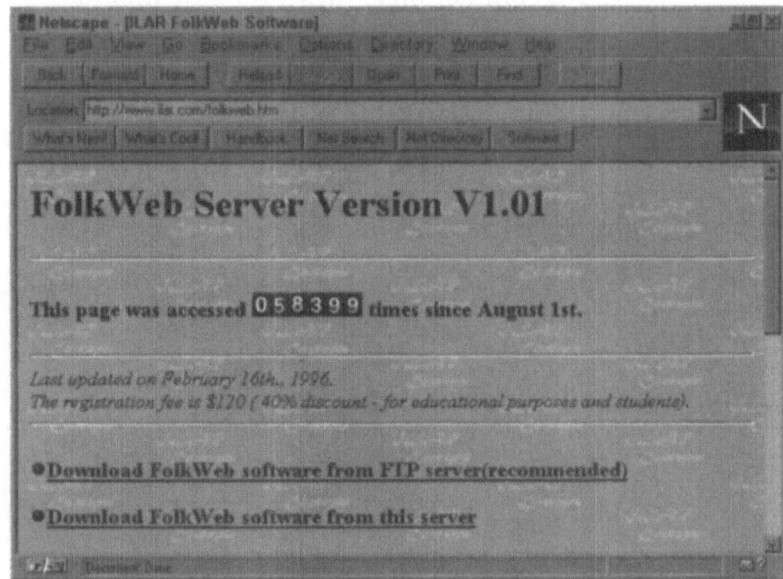

FIGURE 3.11.
FolkWeb.

FIGURE 3.12.
SAIC-HTTP.

able via a graphical administration and file security system. The ODBC connection is via server-side includes, which allows for DB query results to be placed inside HTML documents for retrieval by Web clients. Windows NT BackOffice API support allows the creation of Web applications as Windows DLLs, for increased performance. SafetyWeb includes extended log file creation, CGI scripting (a Perl scripting language package is included), and an HTML editing suite, HoTMetaL Pro. A set of TCP/IP applications, the Spry InternetOffice suite, is also a part of the package.

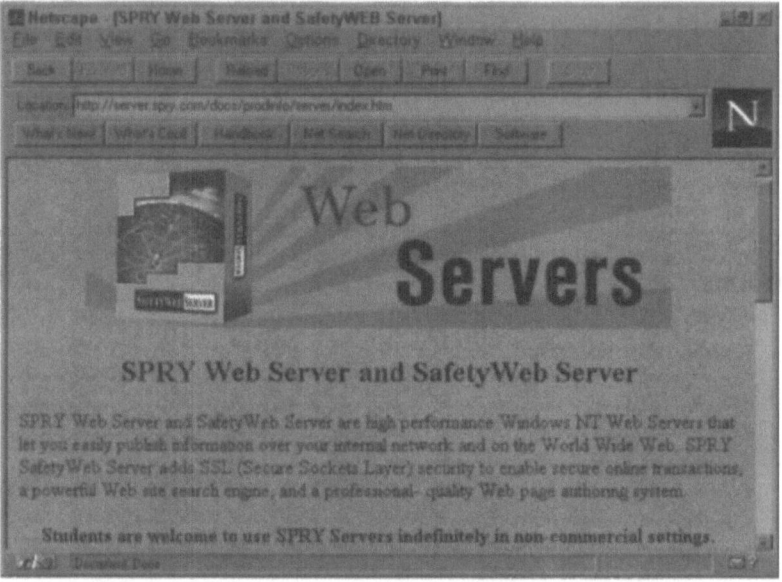

FIGURE 3.13.
Spry SafetyWeb.

Frontier Technology's SuperWeb server's (`http://www.frontiertech.com/products/superweb.htm`) main claim lies in its international support of 14 languages. SSL and S-HTTP security are standard, as are standard user access controls. The graphical administration tool can be run either on the host Web server or from a client PC. CGI support includes predefined back-end services and Web application templates that can be customized for your own Web sites. SuperWeb also includes WebDesigner, an easy-to-use HTML editing application, and HyperCheck, a link-checking tool that verifies hyperlinks in your Web pages automatically.

Luckman's WebCommander (`http://www.luckman.com/wc/webcom.html`) is a complete Website package. It includes graphical setup and administration tools, SSL, S-HTTP, and RSA Public Key security, and real-time performance monitoring (via custom reports and log files). HTML support for CGI scripting via

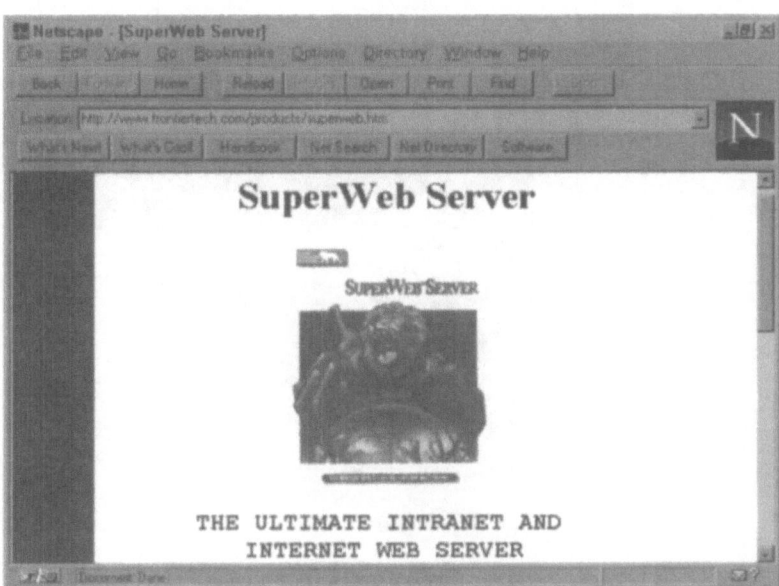

FIGURE 3.14.
SuperWeb.

Perl is also included, and there's a complete WebStudio graphical HTML editing suite with templates and wizards to help you create your Web pages.

WebCommander features the Architext Excite search engine, and database connectivity via an ODBC connection kit (Fig. 3.15). Automatic credit card clearance for digital transactions through national clearinghouses is also built in. Additional features include an SMTP Email server and a 32-bit Enhanced Mosaic Web browser.

WebQuest, from Questar (http://www.Questar.com/), features WebMeister, a graphical Webspace manager (with real-time diagnostics and HTML link validation), and WebEdit, an HTML editor (Fig. 3.16). The WebAdmin tool includes a GUI setup and administration interface with local and remote control. WebQuest supports standard CGI scripting, as well as Server Side Includes Plus (SSI+), for interactive Web applications that can connect to live databases without requiring CGI. ODBC and SMTP Email connectivity is also included, via SSI+.

O'Reilly's WebSite Professional Web server (http://website.ora.com/) includes graphical administration tools like WebView, a directory index and search engine with an integrated HTML link monitor (that reports automatically when it finds broken links). There's also support for standard CGI and Server Side Includes, as well as for a VisualBasic 4 framework via CGI. Security is via SSL and S-HTTP. The HotDog HTML editor can be used to create and maintain Web documents, and a copy of Enhanced 32-

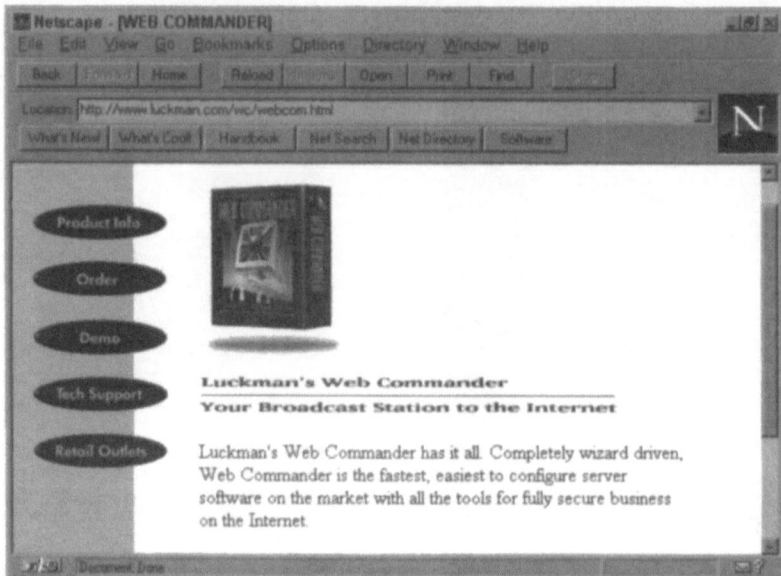

FIGURE 3.15.
WebCommander.

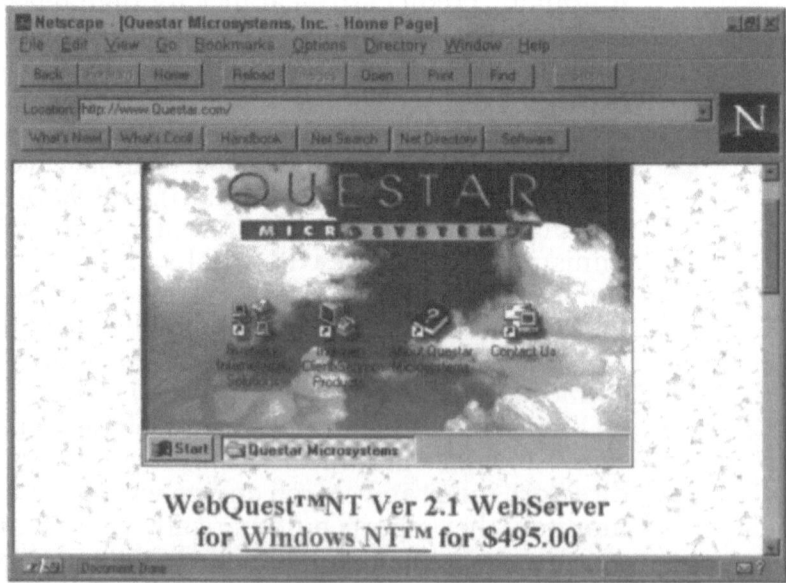

FIGURE 3.16.
WebQuest.

bit Spyglass Mosaic is also included (for browsing your finished pages).

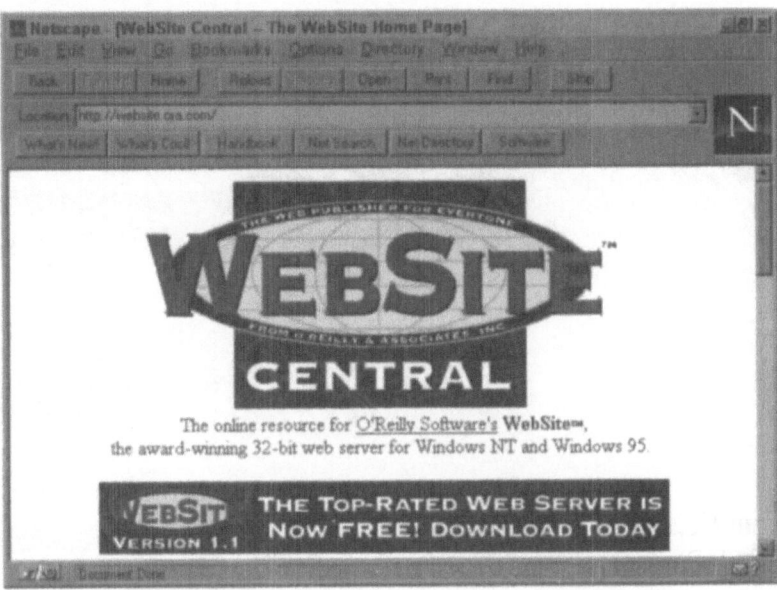

FIGURE 3.17.
WebSite.

WebSTAR, from QuarterDeck (http://www.quarterdeck.com), has a graphical Control Center that makes setting up your Web server a snap (Fig. 3.18). The Control Center handles server administration and HTML document management, and it also includes user access controls and an integrated a log file browser. CGI scripting and image-map control is also supported in WebSTAR.

ZBSoft's ZBServer Pro Secure (http://www.zbserver.com/) features the ZBServer Control graphical setup and maintenance application (Fig. 3.19). There's also a real-time activity monitor, and SSL-S-HTTP security. HTML features include CGI support via Perl, server-side includes and macros, and Java compatibility. ZBServer also includes an integrated Message Board system, and built-in Gopher and FTP file transfer support.

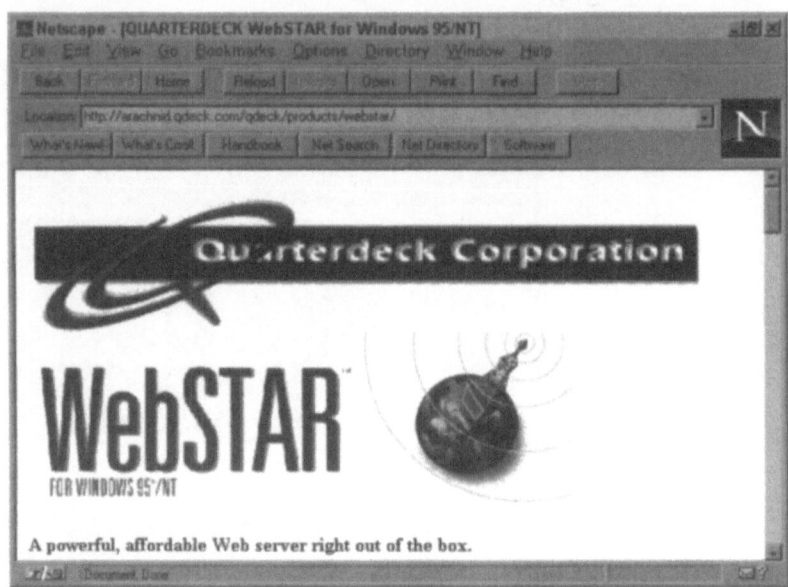

FIGURE 3.18.
WebSTAR.

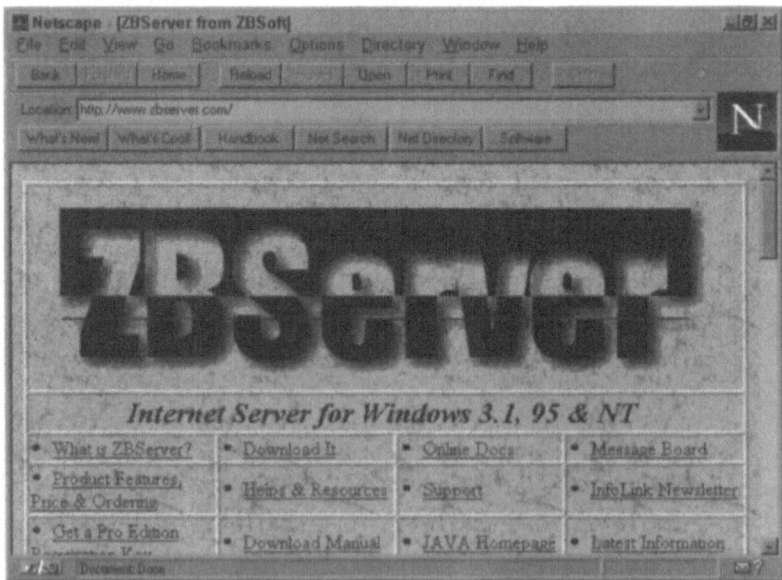

FIGURE 3.19.
ZBServer Pro.

Specialty Products

ExpressO (http://www.capitalcity.com:4321/) is a Web server written entirely in Java. It includes graphical setup and administration tools, and real-time performance monitoring (with several different log file formats). CGI support and image-map handling are built in. The advanced Java compatibility includes Java scripting capabilities that you can use to extend the server's basic functionality. Security is via Basic Authentication (username/password). ExpressO requires the Java run-time software from Sun Microsystems (http://java.sun.com).

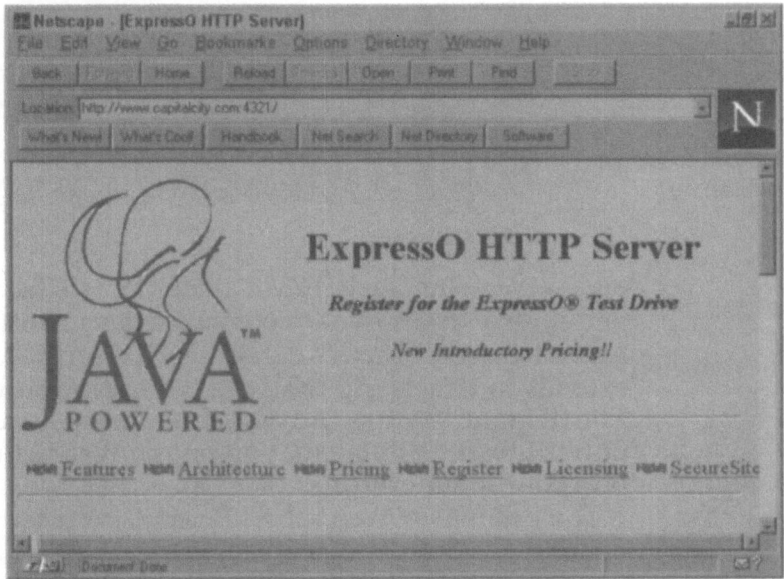

FIGURE 3.20.
ExpressO.

Folio's Professional Web server (http://www.folio.com/) is especially designed to publish Folio Infobase databases on the Web (Fig. 3.21). The basic Web functions include CGI scripting, server-side includes, and image-map support, and security via Basic Authentication (username/password). Gopher and FTP protocols are included. The extended InfoBase connections give the ability to offer Web users the same query structuring and information access tools that are included in the Folio VIEWS InfoBase Manager (for accessing Folio Infobases, of course). A copy of the InfoBase Manager application, used to access the customizable help system, is also included.

The Oracle Web server (http://www.oracle.com) is composed of three elements: the Web Listener, the Web Agent, and the Oracle 7 Workgroup server (Fig. 3.22). The Web Listener GUI front

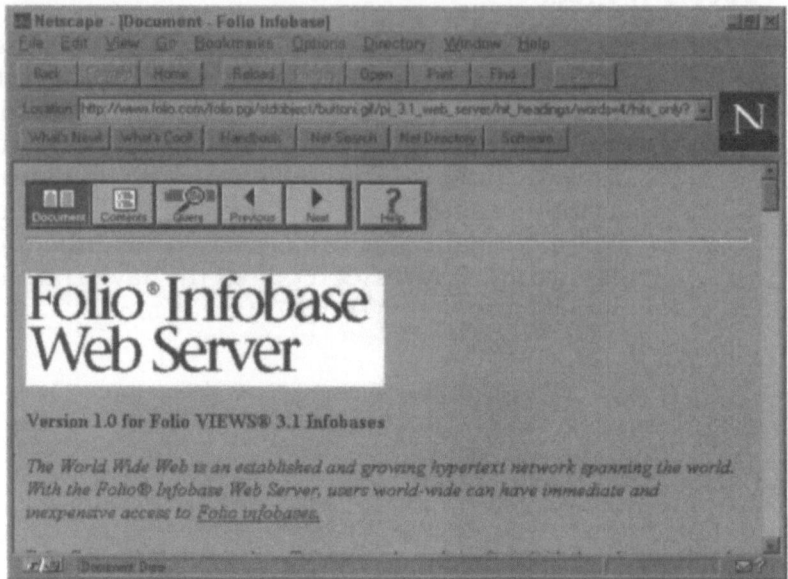

FIGURE 3.21.
Folio Professional
Web server.

end serves standard HTML documents (like any Web server), and it also serves dynamic documents generated from the Web Agent from an Oracle 7 database. CGI scripting is standard, and extends to Oracle PL/ SQL query integration via the WebAgent. The tight integration with Oracle 7 databases allows for dynamic publishing of DB information on the Web using standard stored procedures and routines.

The Spinnaker Web server (http://www.searchlight.com), from Searchlight Software, features a Dynamic HTML extension system that automatically detects the kind of browser your users are connecting with and serves them the proper kinds of files, eliminating browser incompatibility. Spinnaker also features graphical setup and administration tools, and a server-side programming interface, CGI-DLL, that lets programmers write Web applications into the server directly. An example CGI-DLL application is the included Web conferencing system, a BBS public conference system that lets your users interact with each other, and connects to existing Searchlight BBS databases.

WebBase (http://www.webbase.com/) is a database-integrated Web server (Fig. 3.24). It gives programmers the ability to embed DB queries into HTML hyperlinks (like the Oracle WebServer), with support for over 50 database formats (like MS Access and FoxPro, dBase, Oracle, and Paradox). Basic HTML features are also included. It works in stand-alone mode, or in conjunction with another Web server (to provide DB connectivity features).

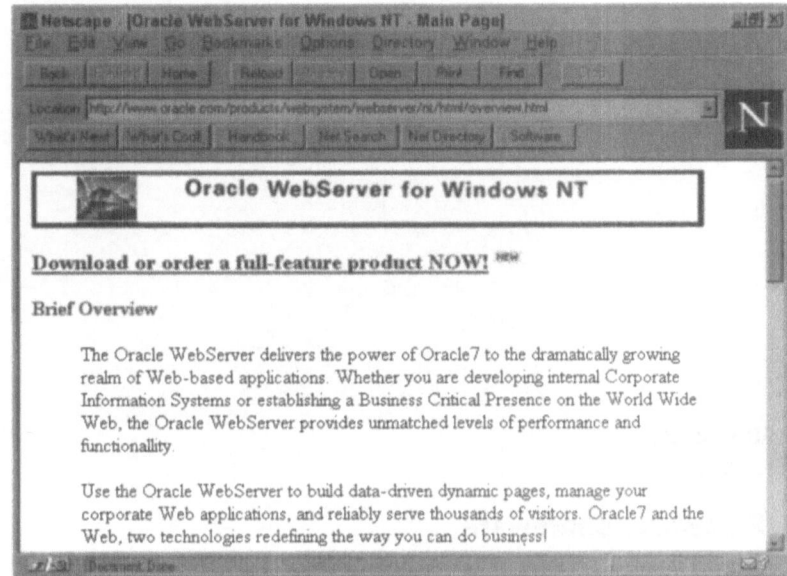

FIGURE 3.22.
Oracle Web server.

FIGURE 3.23.
Spinnaker.

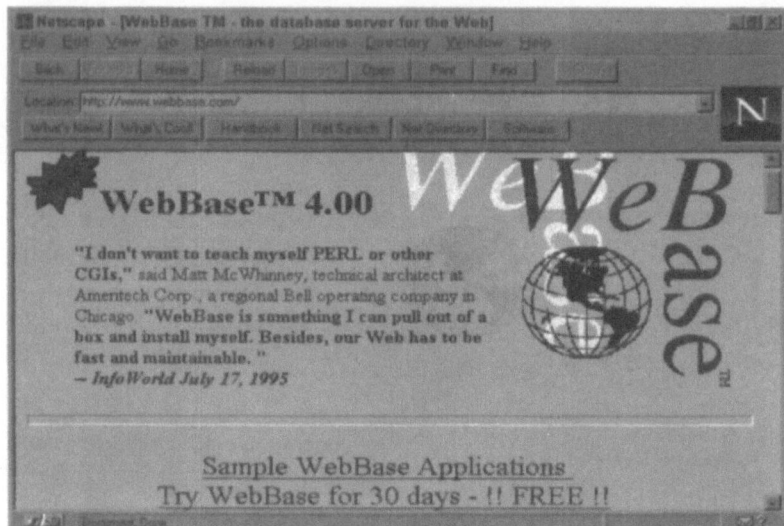

FIGURE 3.24.
WebBase.

Freeware/Shareware

Fnord! (`http://www.wpi.edu/~bmorin/fnord/faq/`) is a freeware NT Web server that includes an easy to use configuration and setup program, Basic Authentication (username/password) security, and transaction log file generation in common formats. There's also CGI scripting and Perl support, for developing interactive Web applications.

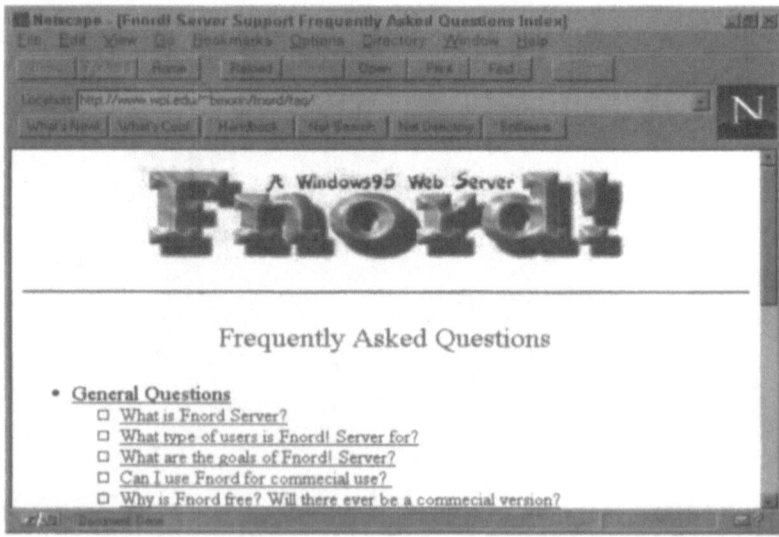

FIGURE 3.25.
Fnord!

4
Web Sites for NT Software

There are a myriad of good sites for NT software on the Net. These include everything from NT Web servers and Internet client programs to applications and configuration utilities. The software linked from these sites include shareware and public domain programs, and beta software from commercial vendors. The NT-related software sites also include links to ancillary support files, NT user groups, press releases and technical information, and general support FAQs (Frequently Asked Questions) from users across the world. You may also find on-line NT conferences and Email discussion groups, and links to Usenet news groups on different NT subjects.

1) The first place to start is at Microsoft. The specific site for the NT client software is the Windows NT Workstation page at the Microsoft Web site (`http://www.microsoft.com/NTWorkstation/`). Here you can find information like product overviews, evaluation tools, technical support, and related resources and services (Fig. 4.1). There are also news and events pages, with information on upcoming releases and beta software availability. You can also see how tightly Microsoft will try to exert control over the reviewing process, with articles that feature the result of "Reviewer's Workshops" (where Microsoft will attempt to lead supposedly impartial reviewers in their evaluations on NT); *caveat lector* is in effect, certainly. There's enough information here in other sections for you to make your own decisions.

You might find the Planning, Migration, and Deployment pages

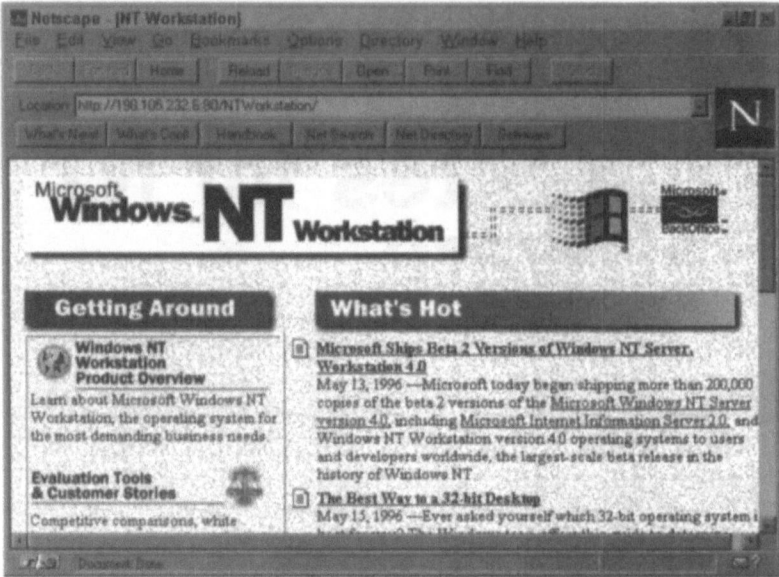

FIGURE 4.1.
Top level, NT
Workstation page.

useful as well. These feature in-depth looks at topics such as TCP-IP integration, C2 security issues, and enterprise-level support. This is also the section where you'll find sample chapters from the Windows NT Resource Kit (good for gaining a helpful overview of how NT works), as well as hardware compatibility lists, and case studies of companies that have successfully implemented NT in their businesses.

The Free Software link here will lead to a Microsoft support on-line page, with links to downloadable NT software you can use to help configure your system properly. These include printer and video drivers, SCSI utilities, and network software. You can also download disk image files (for making floppy-based installation software) of current NT service packs, which include an assortment of updated drivers and related files.

The Microsoft Back Office Web site (http://www.microsoft.com/backoffice/) is where you'll find information on the integrated network product family that centers around Windows NT Server (Fig. 4.4). This is a good stop to find out more about these products. The Back Office top page features links to pages for NT Server, the Internet Information Server, mail and database server products, and system management tools. There are also news and press announcements, evaluation tools (and Microsoft-influenced performance results), and related promotional material.

See the Windows NT Server page (http://www.microsoft.com/NTServer/) for a direct look at the operating system, including product overviews, technical support and related resource links,

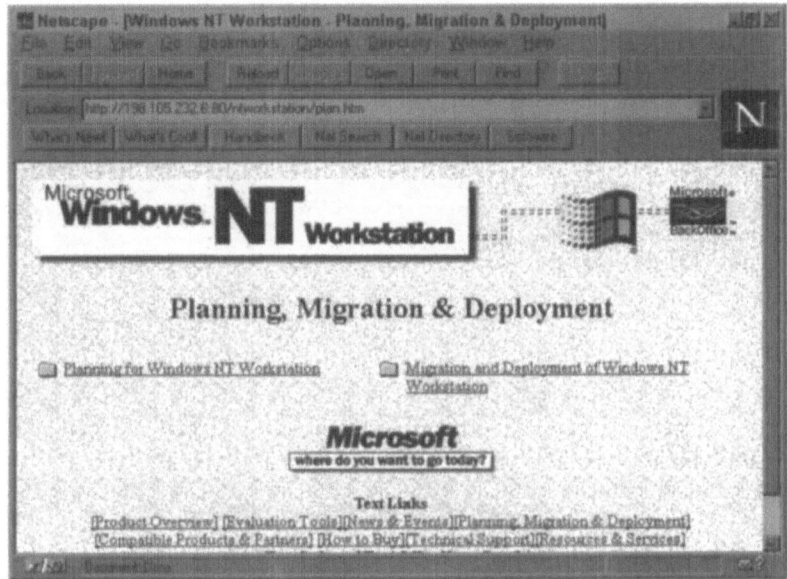

FIGURE 4.2.
Planning and
Migration Page.

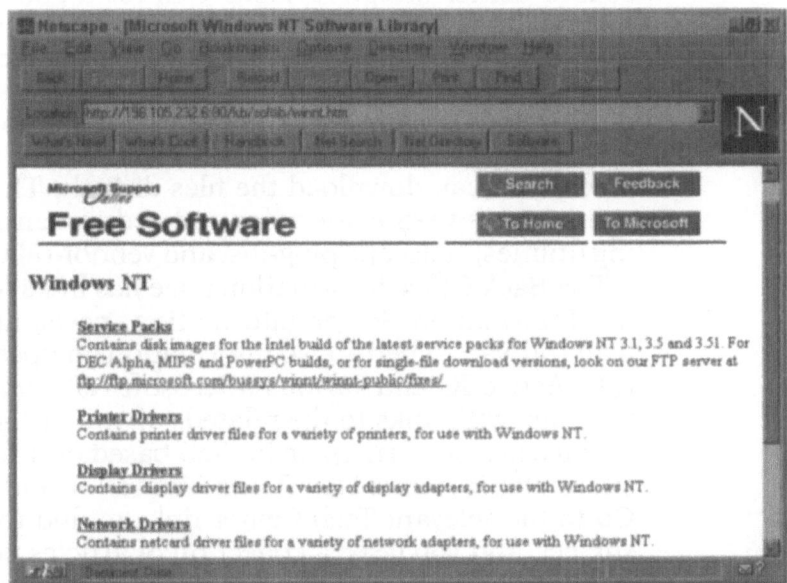

FIGURE 4.3.
Free software page.

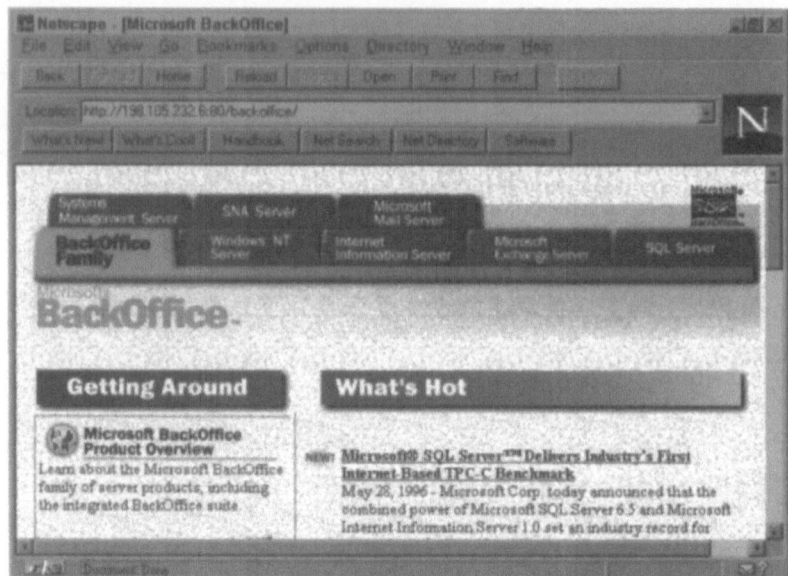

FIGURE 4.4.
MS Back Office top page.

and press releases (Fig. 4.5). There's also a migration planning guide area, and a section for small business resource information. It's a lot of information, and it helps to keep the operating system in perspective.

2) You may also want to try the Beverly Hills Software NT Resource Center (`http://www.bhs.com`) for a good collection of NT information, including links to downloadable software, interactive user forums, news reports, and related Web sites.

The Applications section is where you'll find a good collection of NT-related shareware and related files. The most recent programs are featured in a table format, with links to the places where you can download the files directly. There are also more comprehensive directories for updated system drivers, Perl scripting utilities, Netscape plug-ins, and vendor-related files (Fig. 4.7).

The Back Office information page has links to Microsoft Internet Information Server information, news, and downloadable beta software. There's also information on upcoming technology (like Active X) and various Microsoft NT Server software components, with links to the related software (Fig. 4.8).

You can also participate in Web-based user forums at the BHS site, on topics related to NT administration and end user support. Go to the relevant Tech Center links to find the forum for your subject, and you'll see a collection of articles posted on separate subjects. You can scan the lists to see if your specific question is being answered, or post your own query (Fig. 4.9).

FIGURE 4.5.
MS NT Server page.

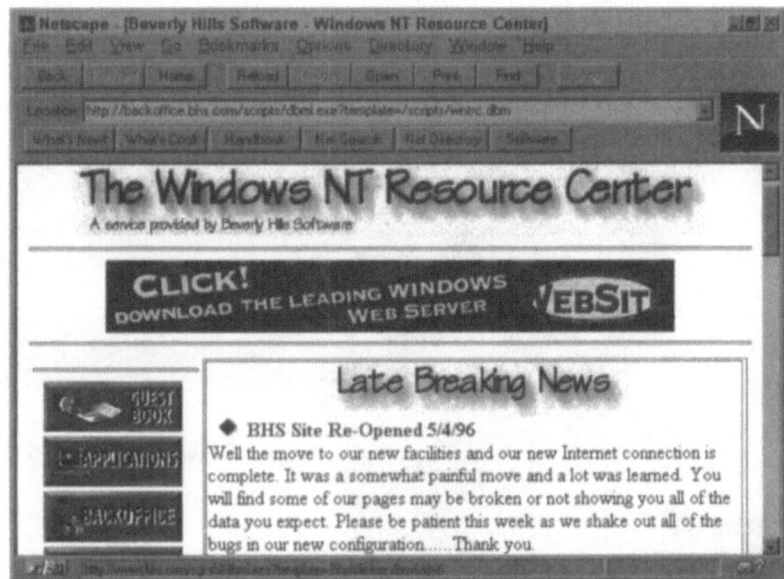

FIGURE 4.6.
Top Page, BHS.

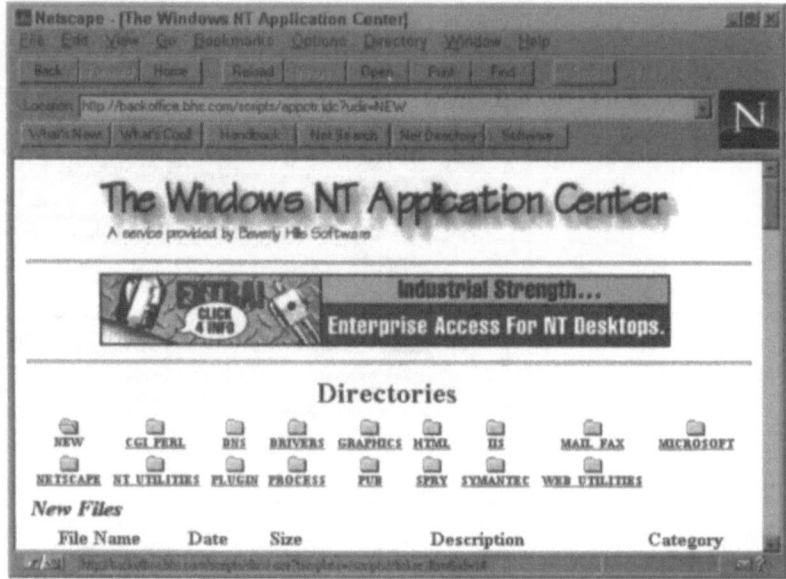

FIGURE 4.7.
Applications section,
BHS.

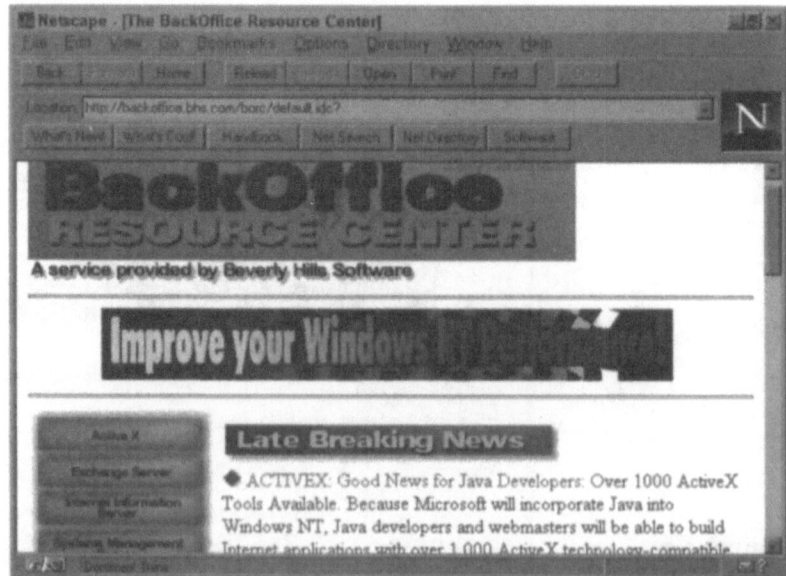

FIGURE 4.8.
BHS Back Office
page.

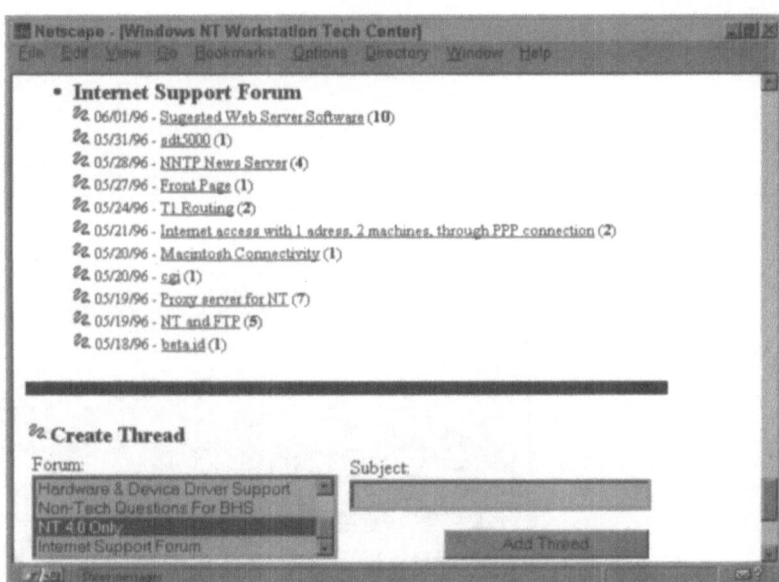

FIGURE 4.9.
BHS Forum shot.

3) The sister site to the Beverly Hills Software NT Resource Center is the iNformaTion site (`http://www.rmm.com/nt/`), a huge collection of links to NT software, information, and related resources. Check out the FTP-Application and Download sections for places to find software for your system, as well as the areas with FAQs on NT-related topics, and links to Internet mailing lists on the same subject. The site also features a good list of links to on-line NT publications, Web site maintainer utilities, and security/virus information (Fig. 4.10).

4) The Sam Houston State University Self-Reported Windows NT Links site (`http://coba.shsu.edu:88/messages/nt-list.htm`) is an ever-growing annotated list of NT-related sites and Web servers from everywhere on the planet. There are also links to NT Usenet newsgroups and on-line Windows NT Internet FAQs, software resources and tools, and application demonstrations. Also be sure to check out the links to NT User Group Web sites; there may be a group in your area, with member benefits like technical support. You can add your own NT site links to the categories listed here as well (Fig. 4.11).

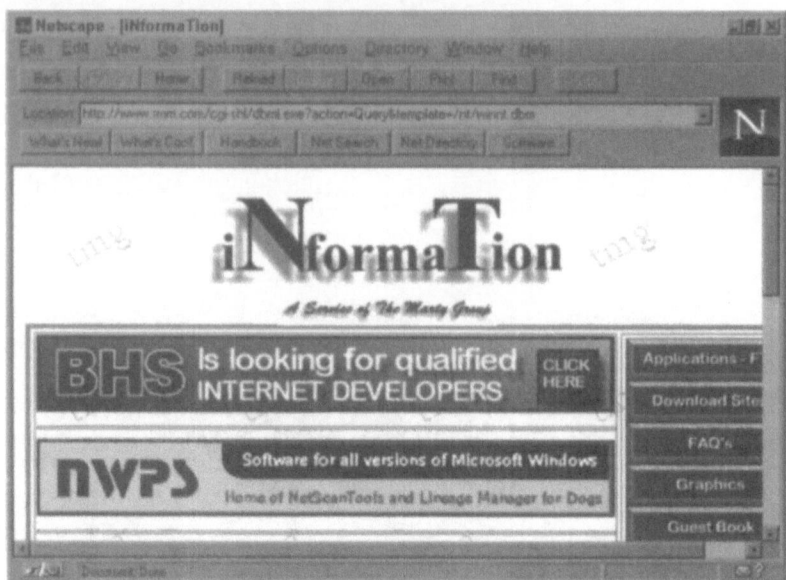

FIGURE 4.10.
iNformaTion main page.

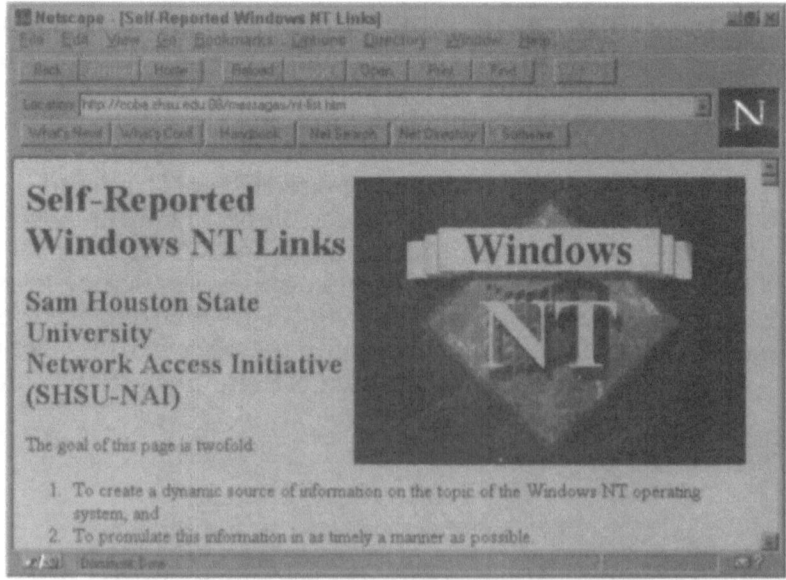

FIGURE 4.11.
SHS main page.

5) The Distance Learning Laboratories' NT Web Developers' Resources site (`http://stargate.con-ed.howard.edu/Webpages/dll/Resources/default.htm`) is a good collection of available resources for Web development on Windows NT. It is not specifically Microsoft-centric, and gives a good look at what's also out there. There are links to several of the main Web server vendors, including freeware from EMWAC, as well as sites for commercial NT Web server software from Open Text, Microsoft, Netscape, Process Software, Spyglass, and O'Reilly.

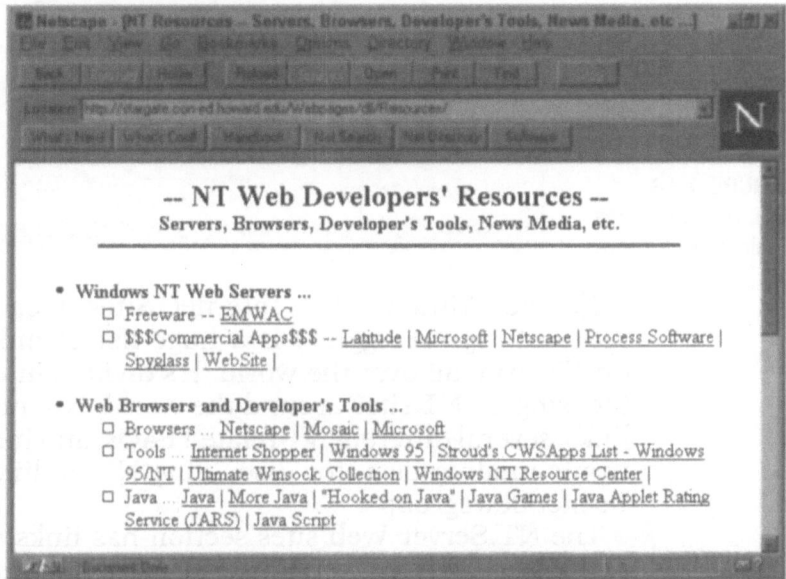

FIGURE 4.12.
DLL NT Resources
main page top.

There are also a lot of good links to Web browser software and utilities for developing Web pages. Here you'll find direct links to Microsoft's Internet Explorer, Netscape Navigator, and NCSA Mosaic, a brief list of sites with resources for Windows NT on the Internet, and a lot of Java links. The Developing Web Pages section features links to sound effects, backgrounds, pictures, and clip art, as well as tutorial info, and good links to places where you can publicize your Web site across the Internet. You'll also find a strong selection of links to the best search engines on the Net, and a short list of good Internet information resources (major publishers and government sites).

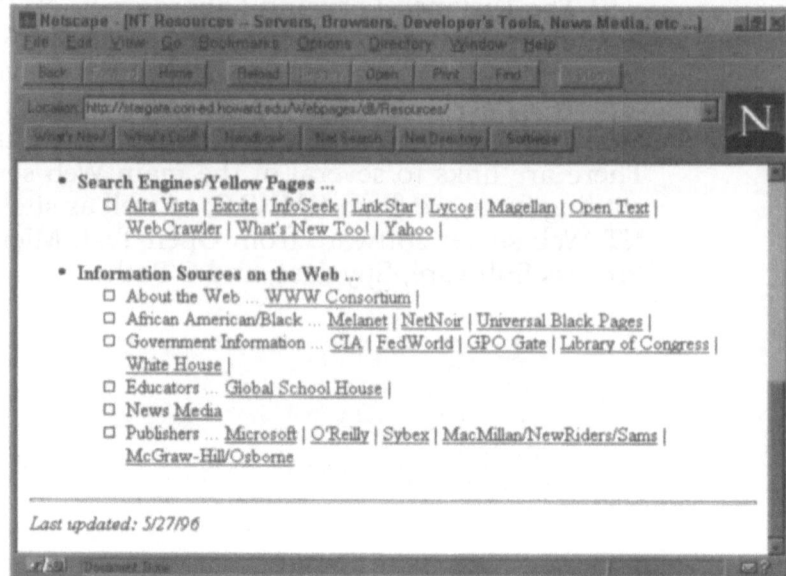

FIGURE 4.13.
DLL NT Resources
main page bottom.

6) The Windows NT Internet Sites Web site (`http://www.frogpond.org/~sscoggin/`) is a huge list of links to information on NT from all over the world. It's divided into several sections, focusing on NT sites around the world, comprehensive FTP site links, several different NT-related FAQs, and information on electronic mailing lists (for discussing NT on-line) and searchable Usenet newsgroups.

The NT Server Web sites section has links to Web site applications and services information, HTML writing guides, and related utilities. There's also a section with a huge set of links to NT files from several sites, including FTP and gopher servers and NT Web resource centers.

You can also plow through a long list of User Group sites (both real and proposed, with contact information for each group). Following this section are resources for miscellaneous information on NT and Internet software products, Web sites, tech support centers, and hardware information. This site may be a little hard to navigate, but the information here is extensive, and can make the effort worthwhile. Try the Edit/Find command in your browser to look up specific information on the long page.

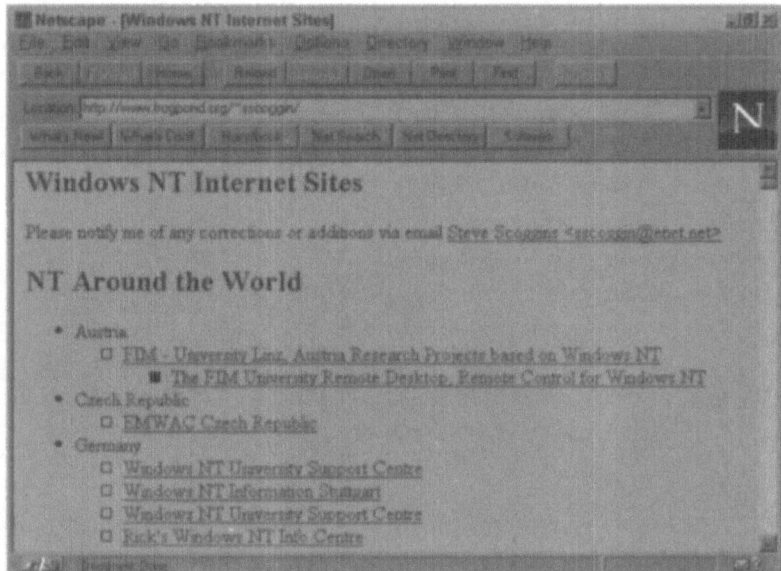

FIGURE 4.14.
NT Internet Sites
main page.

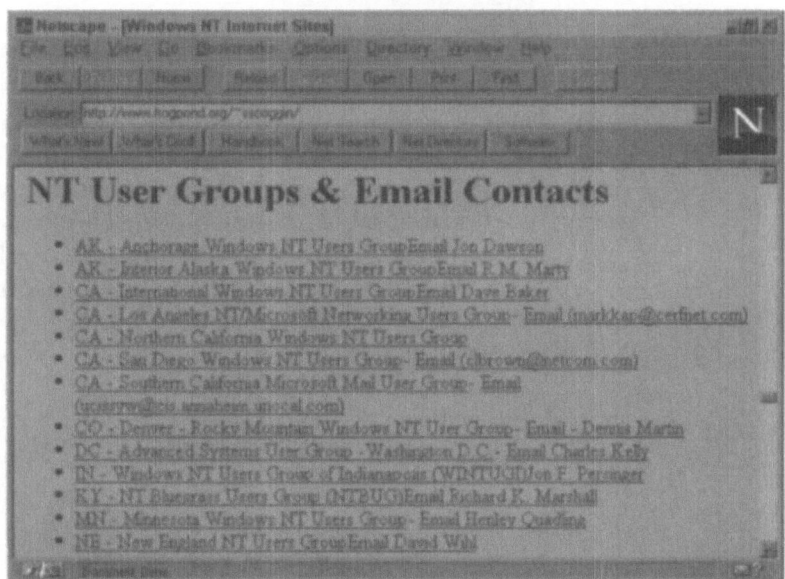

FIGURE 4.15.
NT Internet Sites
mid-page.

7) Sanjaya's Windows NT Resource Center (`http://wonderland.dial.umd.edu/NT/`) is an interesting place, filled with the site maintainer's own lists of favorite NT utilities (with links), helpful NT tips and tricks, and information on how to set up NT Internet services (in the Windows NT-related Network, WWW, and Internet resources section). There are also links to interesting hardware-related and NT news sites, and an interactive WebBoard messaging system for on-line discussion of NT topics.

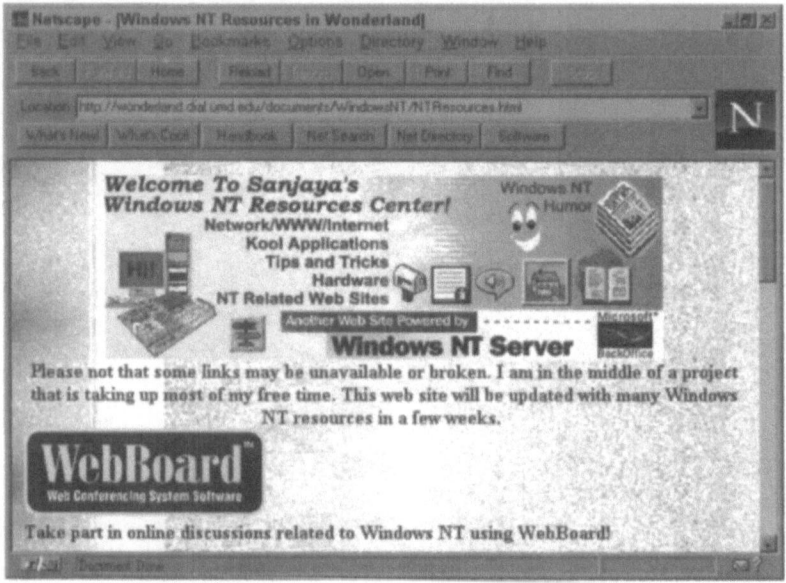

FIGURE 4.16.
Sanjaya main page.

8) The InterGreatWindows NT Universe (at `http://www.intergreat.com/winnt/winnt.htm`) is a definite stop for finding out more about NT on the Net. The sections are very well laid out, and give a lot of good information on NT Web servers, Web setup and design (including links to utilities and applications), general NT-related Web sites, and links to Java resources. In the Windows NT Internet Servers area, you'll find a good table layout of NT Web servers, as well as Email, gopher, DNS, News, and WAIS server software links. Each link has a good basic description of the related software, so you can get a good overall idea of what's on the market (over 19 different Web server packages for NT are listed, for example).

FIGURE 4.17.
InterGreat main
page.

The WWW Server Setup and Design section has links to HTML editors and server-related utilities (like CGI and Perl scripting software), graphics tools and utilities, image map editors, and Web design services. This information is also laid out in a good annotated table format, with ratings. It's a really good collection of software for NT users who need to handle their Web site design and HTML tasks efficiently (Fig. 4.18).

9) SimTel's Coast To Coast Windows NT Software Collection (http://www.coast.net/SimTel/#NT) is a more general NT software resource. There are a lot of file areas here, with directories listed alphabetically, and you can download the programs listed here directly from this site. These include sections for NT administration programs, communications and archive utilities, graphics and business applications, RAS (MS Remote Access) support and utility files, and Internet applications. You can also perform a limited search of the NT Collection, and browse the latest files added to the archive directly.

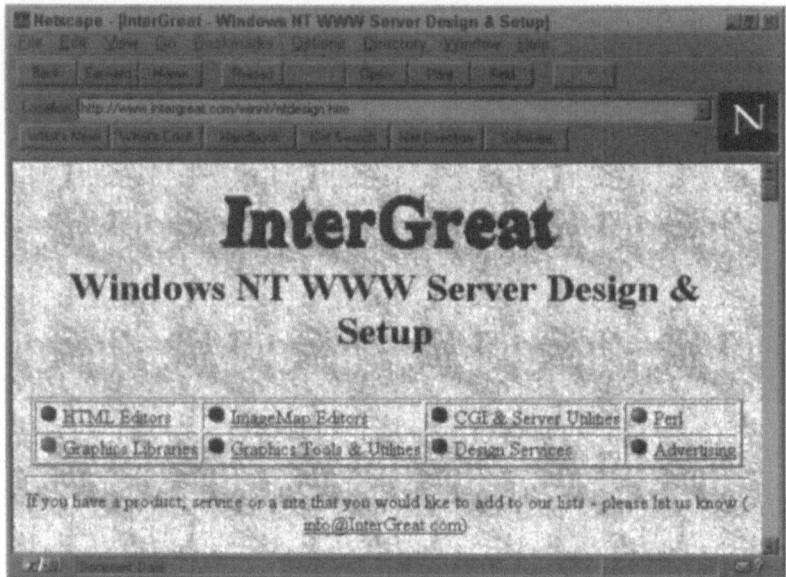

FIGURE 4.18.
InterGreat NT Setup
and Design page.

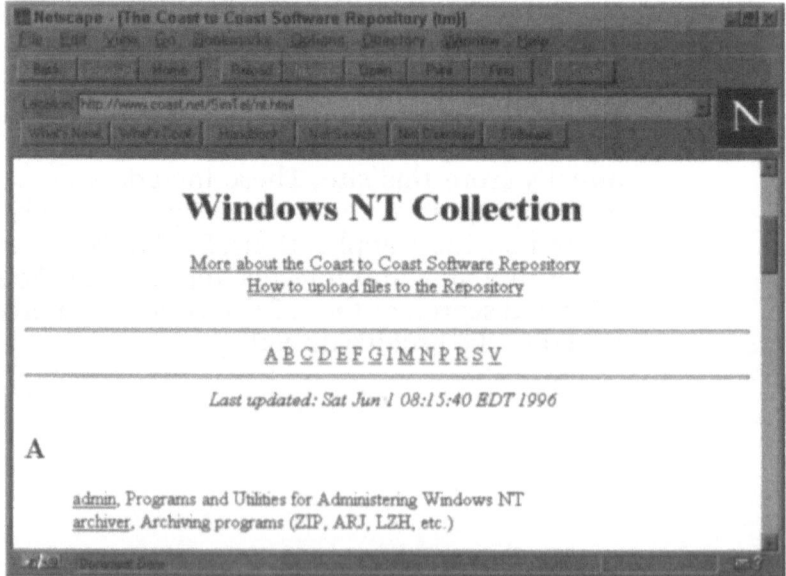

FIGURE 4.19.
SimTel main page.

10) Rick's Windows NT Info Center (`http://rick.wzl.rwth-aachen.de/rick/`) is another hopping site for NT information. This place has great sections for NT news (look here for the latest information on NT Web tools), links to separate Microsoft Web pages arranged by topic, NT user home pages, and software downloading sites. There's also a good selection of FAQs, Hardware Compatibility Lists (HCLs), and Microsoft Knowledge Base documents from across the Web. The Knowledge Base is where Microsoft's technical information on NT and related material is stored, and you can use the links here to browse it directly or search for topics of interest.

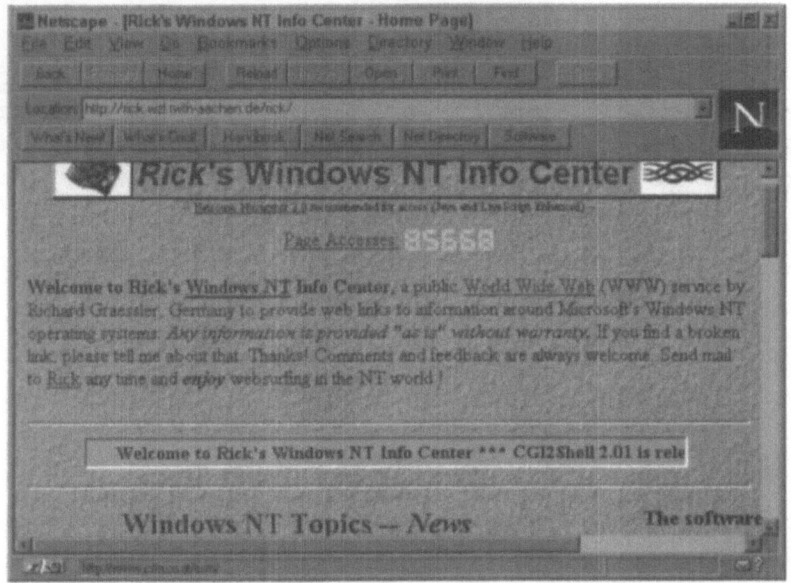

FIGURE 4.20.
Rick's main page.

Also look for the links to on-line newsletters and newsgroups, technical white papers, and Web publishing links. The big NT download area is also represented by a software download area, devoted to companies and sites that have their own Web sites. There's a lot of software linked here, including antivirus and archive utilities, backup software, and NT development tools, specific Web tools like Internet server and client programs and scripting software, and NT drivers, RAS, and Registry utilities.

An interesting addition to Rick's site is the AddURL page, where you can browse a list of NT-related Web sites that's generated by Web users alone, or add your own (Fig. 4.21). There's also an on-line Chat link, where you might be able to talk to the Webmaster in real time (if he's there!).

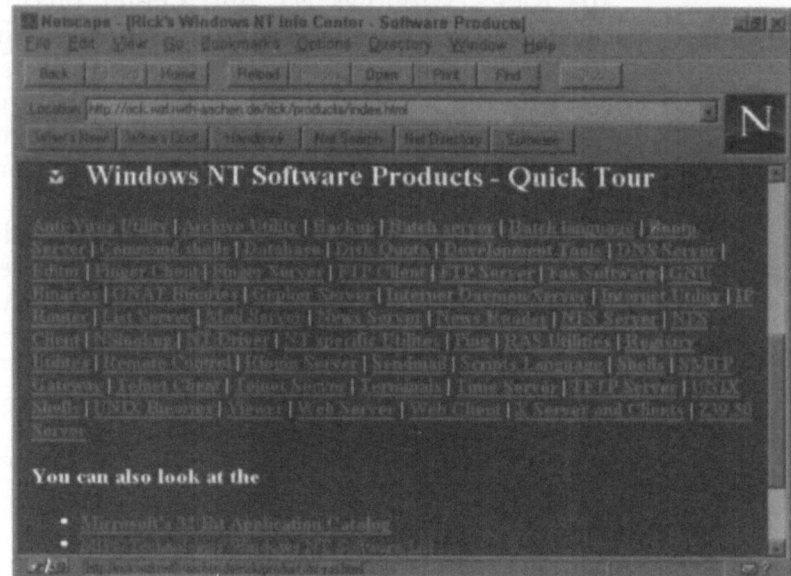

FIGURE 4.21.
Rick's software
page.

5
Web Sites for NT Hardware

Why choose NT software for Web servers and browsers? In the case of running a Web server, the main issue is scalability. NT is designed to run as a multithreaded microkernel operating system, and that means that it can distribute its running processes more efficiently through the hardware that it runs on. NT will run efficiently on Pentium systems, but it's also capable of running on fast RISC processors like DEC Alpha, MIPS, and PowerPC. The scalability issue is tied to the Web server. A Web site with a huge number of connections per day will require more horsepower from the system CPU as the software attempts to handle the connections. NT on Pentium and RISC also scales to multiprocessor systems that can handle large commercial Web site traffic.

Hardware Platforms and Compatibility

Windows NT is a fairly complex operating system, and even though Microsoft claims it can run on almost any PC, you should check the Hardware Compatibility List (HCL) sites carefully to see if you meet the minimum preferred configuration. Fortunately, Microsoft does go a long way to providing a high level of support for the hardware associated with NT.

The main HCL site at Microsoft (`http://www.microsoft.com/NTServer/hcl/hclintro.htm`) is updated frequently, and has sections for certified computer systems (for Intel and RISC-based computers), peripherals (video, SCSI, communications, printers), and technical information. You can also download the HCL document directly, to use off-line (in Word for Windows format). Compatibility lists for NT 4.O should be close to the same for NT 3.5.1; older versions of the HCL are available for users with 3.5.1 NT systems.

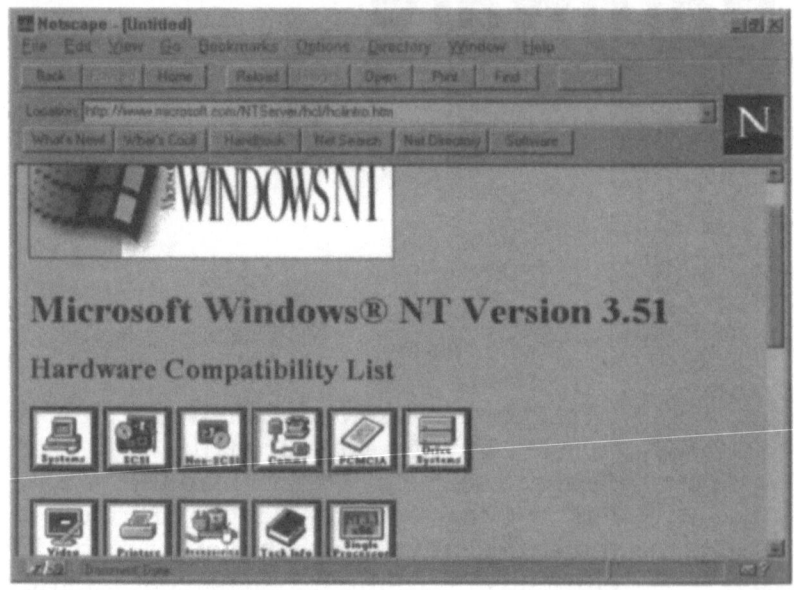

FIGURE 5.1.
Hardware
Compatibility List.

The HCL list is also distributed across the Internet at several different Web sites, in slightly different format. It's essentially the same list. Make sure you check the date of the HCL that you're viewing to ensure that it's the current one. Another good resource of Microsoft's hardware compatibility list is that it's linked to the relevant drivers you may need to get your system up and running, or to ensure that your upgrade parts will work properly with NT.

The Digital Windows NT Info Center (`http://www.windowsnt. digital.com`) features information on Digital's line of NT workstations and servers. These are available with standard Intel processors or RISC-based Alpha CPUs, from desktop configurations to subnotebooks. DEC sells its systems with NT preloaded, and provides support for configuring systems to your specific needs. The NT Info Center Web site also features general NT resource links (user groups, DEC partner sites, software archives), technical white paper archives, and Alpha system drivers and firmware upgrade links.

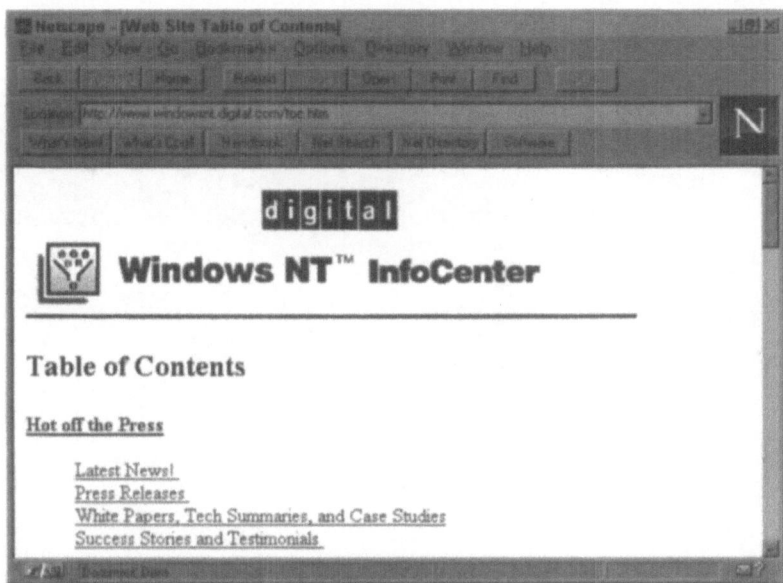

FIGURE 5.2.
DEC Win NT Info
Center.

Intel is a good booster of NT as the operating system of choice for high-end Pentium systems. You can find out more about this type of hardware at the Intel Web site (http://www.intel.com). Try the local search engine linked at the top of the main page to look for NT information directly. This will return a set of links to the NT information distributed about the site. We found links to hardware manufacturers, technical support documents, NT-related hardware press releases, and general FAQs here. There are also case studies of companies using Intel hardware and Windows NT for high-demand Web-related business projects (like Microsoft!). You can also try searching for specific NT subjects that relate to NT here (Fig. 5.3).

PC hardware vendors also have good Web sites. Dell's home page (http://www.dell.com) provides information on the Power-Edge series of Intel-based based NT Web Servers, as well as other NT-certified Dell computer systems. The site also features information on custom hardware configurations, technical support, and customer services. Use the search page to look up information directly. You can also order systems on-line, and check your order status directly from here (Fig. 5.4).

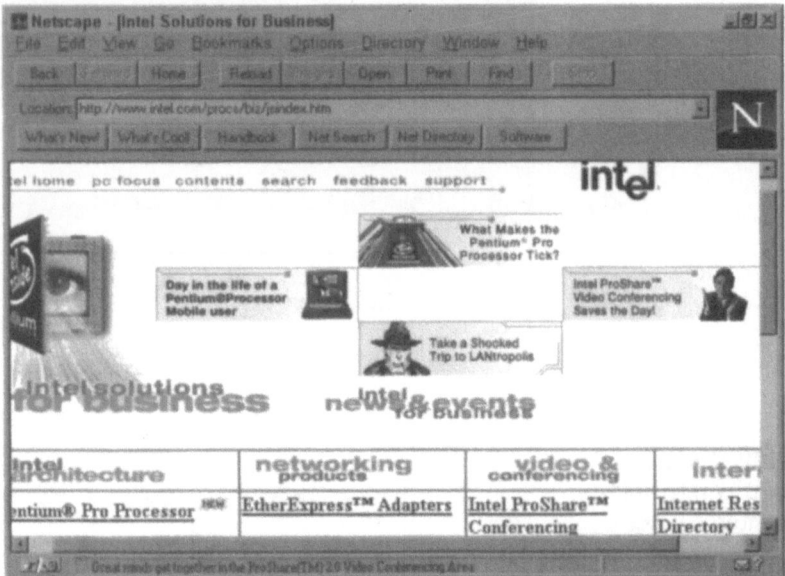

FIGURE 5.3.
Intel Web site.

FIGURE 5.4.
Dell Web site.

Compaq's site (http://www.compaq.com) has information on the ProLiant line of NT servers and Presario NT desktop systems. There are also case studies of Compaq/NT in business use, corporate information, and current press releases. See the Service and Support section for links to support files, drivers and system patches, technical publications, and information on customer support. You can also search the site to find specific answers to your hardware questions, and request technical support FAX documents to be sent directly from the site from a large on-line catalog.

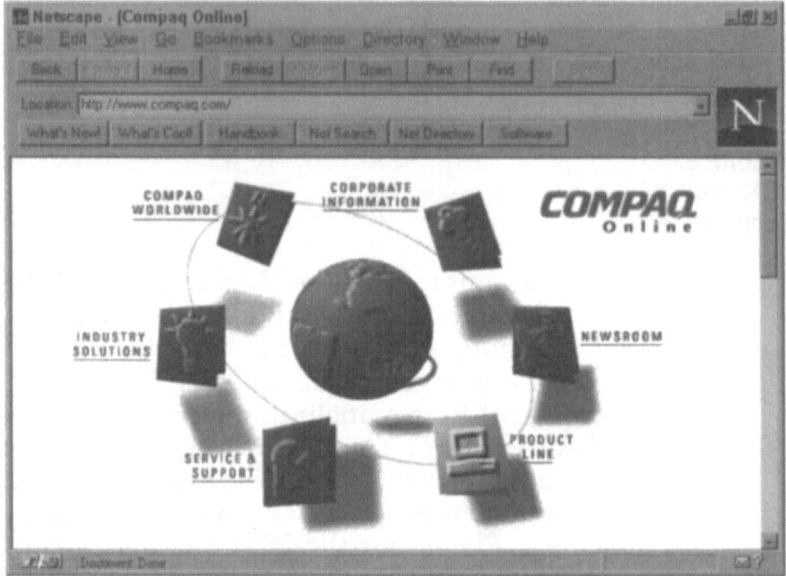

FIGURE 5.5.
Compaq Web site.

The AT&T-NCR NT Support site (http://www.attgis.com/support/nt/ntinfo.htm) is where you'll find information on running NT on AT&T GIS computer systems. This site is divided into sections on integrated software for Windows NT, including NCR products and support aids and NT Fixes files, and an overview of the NCR computer product line. There's also an NT FAQ, and a troubleshooting guide (to help you pinpoint specific problems). Further links will take you to related NT support pages at Microsoft and NCR, and there are also technical support phone numbers you can use to reach NT support analysts for your registered AT&T-NCR computer system.

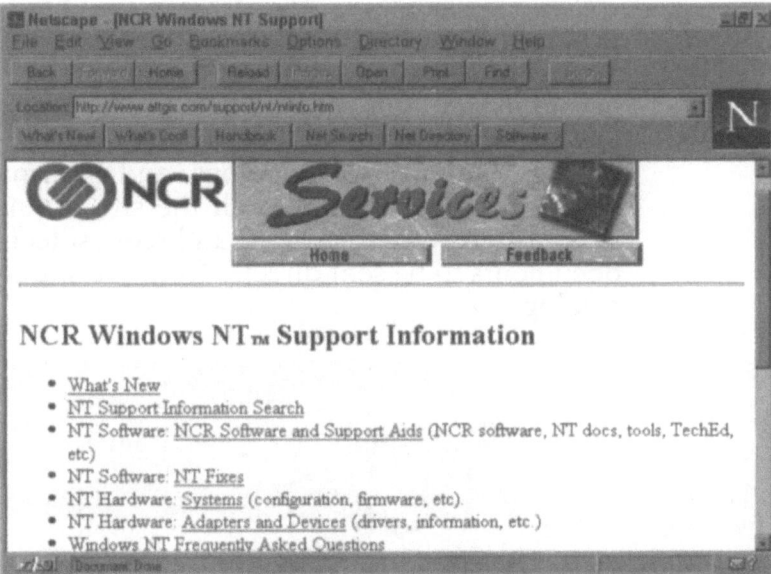

FIGURE 5.6.
AT&T-NCR NT
support site.

You'll want to keep the Hewlett-Packard Web site (http://www.hp.com) handy even if you don't have a Vectra or NetServer system running NT. This is the best place to find support information on the large number of HP printers, plotters, and scanning equipment in use, including technical documents and updated software drivers. The HP site also has a good amount of information on their own NT-capable systems, including technical support newsletters and file archives for updated drivers and system patches. Check out the HP Software Depot for a good link to the On-Demand Support area, a database with a wide range of technical information files, service request documents, and engineering notes that you can search directly.

For a look into NT on RISC computing systems, try the MIPS NT site (http://www.mips.com/windows_nt/Win_NT.html). This site has links to the main vendors of RISC computers that run Windows NT today, including NEC Technologies, Siemens Nixdorf, and UniMicro Systems. There's also a good list of approved 32-bit software that has business applications for NT on MIPS, with links to the relevant vendors. See the MIPS RISC Windows NT Performance Brief for an in-depth look at how RISC processors outperform conventional processors. You can also use the links at the bottom of the main page to find out more about MIPS and its line of processor products.

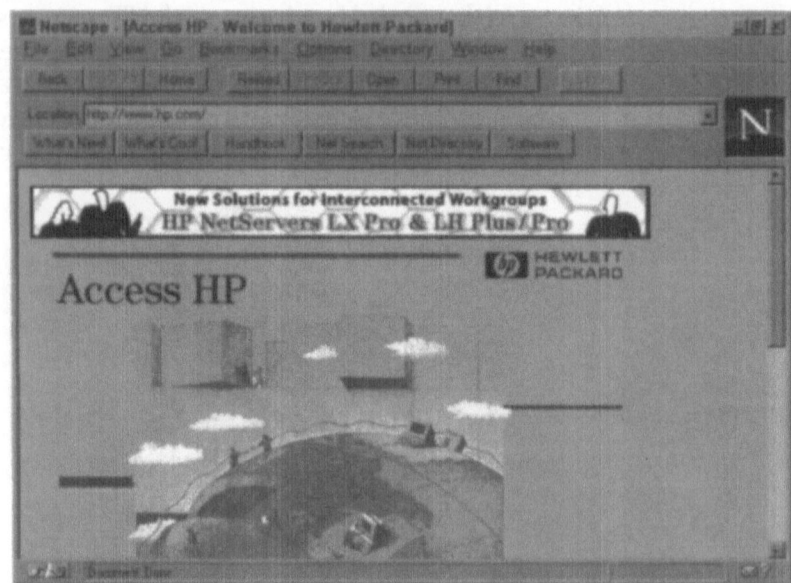

FIGURE 5.7.
HP Web site.

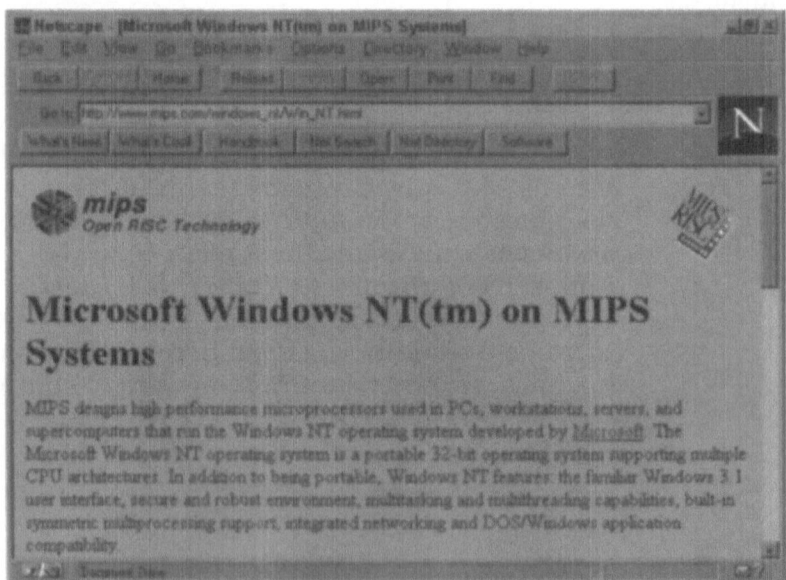

FIGURE 5.8.
MIPS Web site.

Tangent has a Web page devoted solely to supporting NT customers (`http://www.tangent.com/ntfiles/home.htp`). This site has
sections with good descriptions of NT server systems available
from Tangent (Pentium single and multiprocessor systems), as
well as links to NT hardware drivers, software directories, and
NT help files. There are also direct links to related Microsoft software upgrades and patch files, and NT Web server support sites.

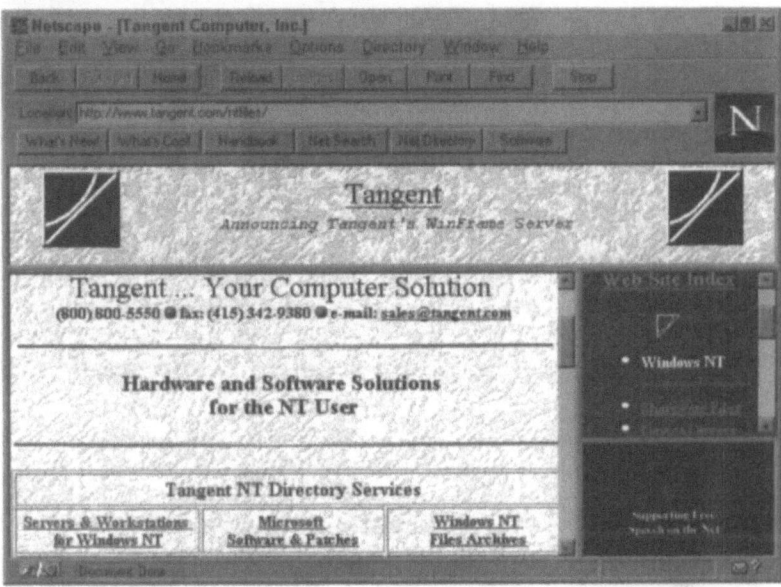

FIGURE 5.9.
Tangent site.

The NEC site (`http://www.nec.com`) is fun to visit, and has a
good collection of information on the RISCserver series of RISC-
based NT server systems, and the ProServa Pentium-based NT
systems. You can go directly to this information by searching for
"windows nt" at the main page. This will return a list of on-line
product brochures and press releases, as well as links to technical
support FAQs and directories for NEC RISC support files (system
drivers and upgrades). You can also use the NEC Comparabase to
get a side-by-side look at the different NT servers that NEC offers.
Just pick the server systems you want to compare, and you'll get
a table showing the different relative technical and performance
specifications.

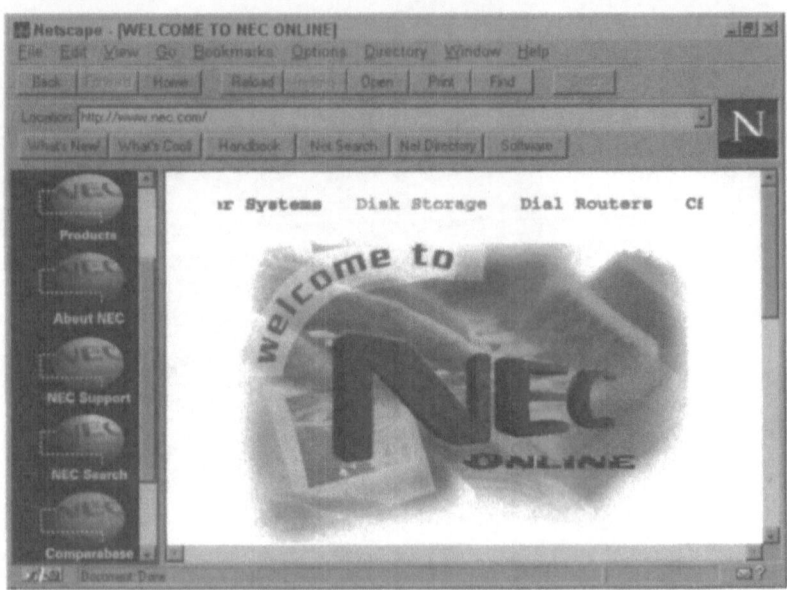

FIGURE 5.10.
NEC home page.

You may have to dig around the Siemens Nixdorf site to find the Windows NT information, but it's there. Try the Midrange Business Systems page (`http://www.sni.de/public/mr/offers/offers.htm`) for links to information on the Siemens RISC server platforms, including product descriptions and technical specifications. You can also search for Windows NT topics across the larger Siemens Nixdorf site. This will return links to more hardware technical support and overview documents, as well as information on NT software certified in Siemens' Middleware catalogs (Fig. 5.11).

Motorola co-developed the PowerPC CPU with IBM and Apple, and is currently bringing out the Common Hardware Reference Platform, PowerPC-based computer systems that will run several operating systems, including Windows NT. The Motorola PowerPC home page (`http://www.mot.com/SPS/PowerPC/`) has a comprehensive overview of the PPC architecture, as well as information on PPC hardware details (`http://www.mot.com/SPS/PowerPC/library/technical_papers/compcon/ppc_arc.html`) and a specific page for Windows NT software on PowerPC (`http://www.mot.com/SPS/PowerPC/overview/nt_home.html`). The NT Software page includes Motorola developer support information and links to Microsoft NT-related Web pages. You can also find a good background document on developing Windows NT applications on PowerPC at `http://www.mot.com/SPS/PowerPC/library/technical_papers/nt_dev_apps/nt_dev_apps.html`.

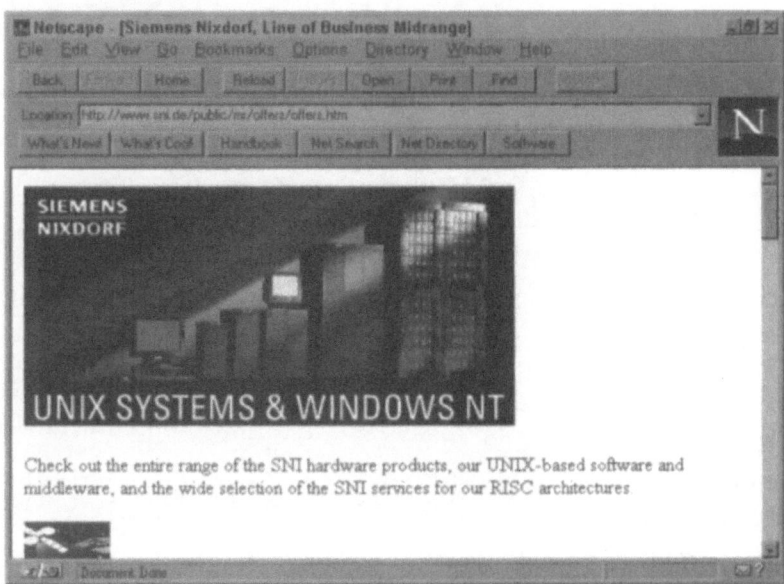

FIGURE 5.11.
Siemens NT Site.

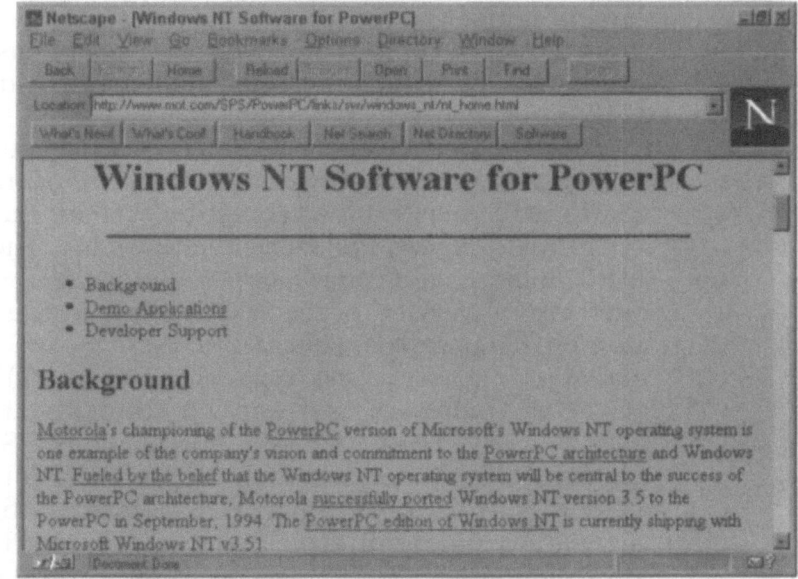

FIGURE 5.12.
Moto PowerPC page.

IBM's Power Series home page (http://www.pc.ibm.com/powerpers/home.html) is where you can find information on PowerPC based workstations and subnotebook ThinkPads that run Windows NT. The site features technical specification sheets, product overviews, and a PowerPC FAQ. You can also find developer program information and lists of vendors with approved software for Power Series PowerPC systems (not all of this is NT software, but the list is growing). Use the search page to find information on NT across IBM's many Web sites. This can get you to service documents, technical support notes, and related file archives.

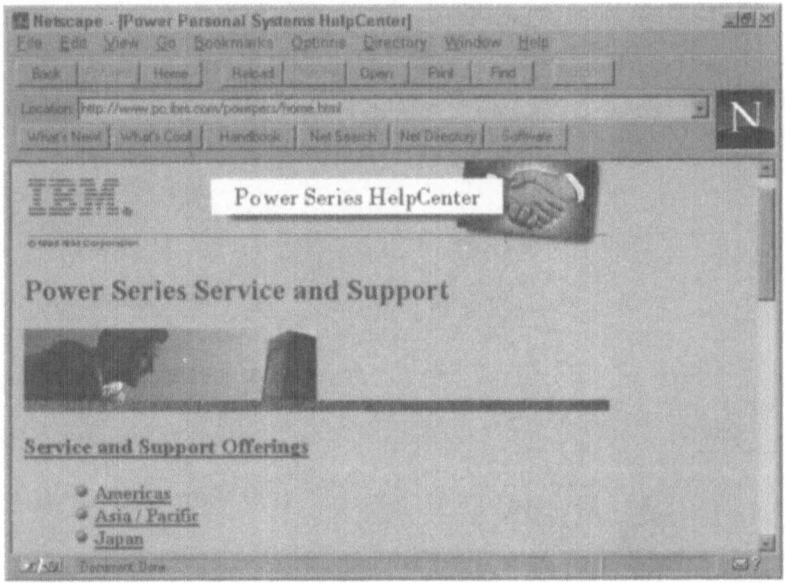

FIGURE 5.13.
IBM PowerPersonal page.

FirePower Systems has an interesting PowerPC-based series of NT workstations. Find out more about them at their colorful site (http://www.firepower.com/). The Product section includes press releases and technical data sheets, as well as information on system configurations and pricing. The Service and Support page lets you request support information right from this Web page, and the Points Of Interest area is a good listing of links to PowerPC-related companies, electronic newsletters, and development efforts (including sites with information on current applications that have been ported to NT on PowerPC).

FIGURE 5.14.
FirePower page.

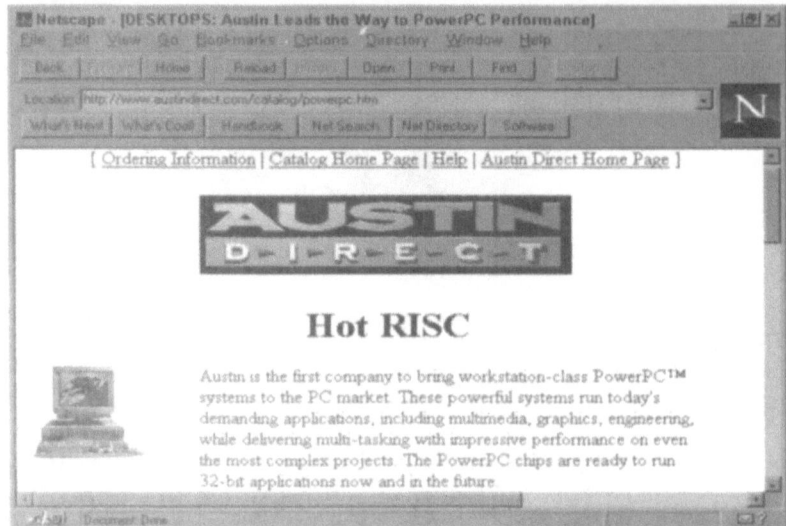

FIGURE 5.15.
Austin page.

Austin Direct (`http://www.ipctechinc.com/`) makes Pentium and PowerPC-based systems that run Windows NT. Their offerings also include fully integrated NT Web server packages. Try the Catalog section to view product information and technical data sheets, and see the Specials area to see what's on sale. There's also a link to an FTP support file archive and a Press Release home page (with information on fast NT Pentium systems and dual-processor PowerPC servers).

6
Java for Windows NT

What is Java? Quite simply, it's the most interesting advance in operating systems, software development, and World Wide Web content to come since the popularization of the Internet. Web sites that are Java-enabled can include interactive applications like stock tickers with live updates, embedded software calculators and charting applications, and sophisticated animation.

Java is a programming language that takes advantage of structured languages of the past, but has been designed to work well with Internet applications (like Web browsers) and Intranet information systems. On the client side, browsers that are Java-enabled can receive Java applets over the Internet (or a local network) in the same way that pictures, text, and sound files are transmitted. These applets are bits of run-time programming code that can take many forms once they reach the browser, including a simple animation to a complex real-time stock charting application. What's more, the Java applets inside the browser can be used like a standard application (if they're sufficiently robust). The stock charting application could include interactive buttons that would change the chart view, for example, or a slider bar that could change how fast the real-time updates would occur.

Netscape Navigator 2.0 and 3.0 are already Java-enabled in their Windows NT versions, and Microsoft is expected to have a Internet Explorer Version 3.0 that is Java-capable soon. This will probably be included with the final release of NT 4.0 Workstation. Sun has also developed the HotJava browser, an independent Java Web browser written in Java itself, with interesting features (like embedded control panels inside the main browser window, and specialized Java support). You can find HotJava at the JavaSoft site, http://java.sun.com.

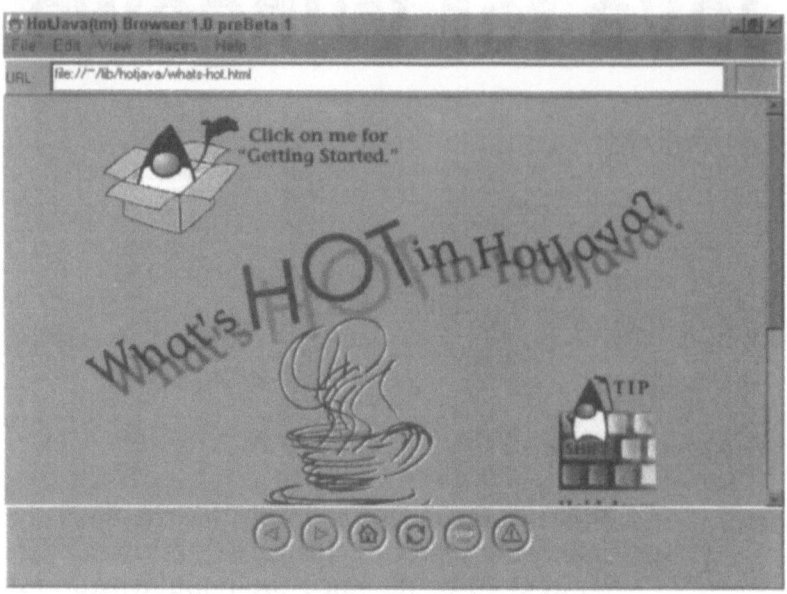

FIGURE 6.1.
HotJava.

It's important to note how much processing power Java applets require. Most Java-enabled Web browsers require a 32-bit operating system, like Windows 95 or NT. The advanced 32-bit nature of Windows NT makes it a better operating system for Java that Windows 95, since NT has been developed from the ground up as a true multitasking environment.

Java Information Sites

JavaSoft, a part of Sun Microsystems, is the company that develops Java. Find out more at their Web site (http://java.sun.com/). The areas linked here include What's Java?, a helpful overview of the Java environment, with FAQs and on-line documentation on specific Java elements, and links to Java-enabled browsers from Netscape (Navigator 2.0) and Sun (HotJava). There's also additional information on Java books, videos, and training materials. Check out the Developer's Corner for in-depth information on Sun's development programs and conferences, and information on Java Workshop and the Java Developers' Kit (JDK), programming environments for use in creating Java applets (with links to downloading sites for the Windows NT versions).

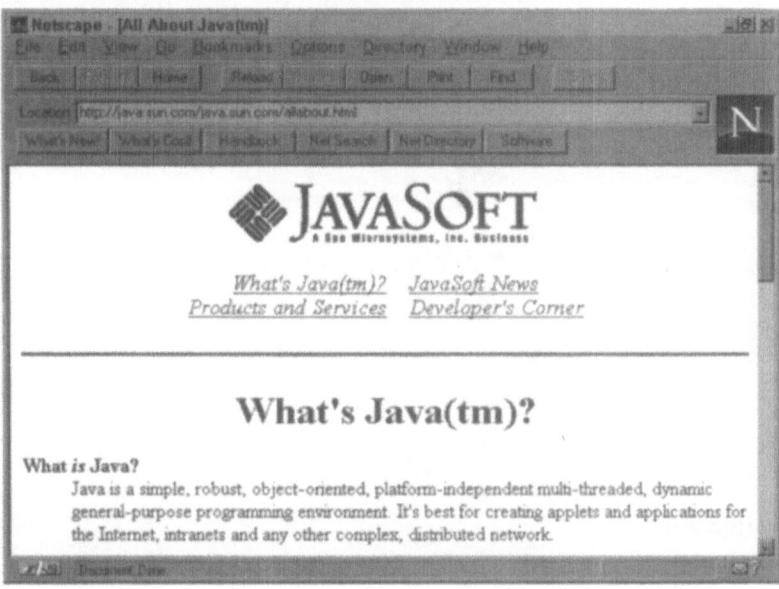

FIGURE 6.2.
JavaSoft.

The Big Kahuna of Java sites, Gamelan (`http://www.gamelan.com`) is the place to find almost anything in the Java universe (Fig. 6.3). See the well-annotated sections for arts and entertainment, business and finance, education, and multimedia, with links to cool Java resources. There are also sections for programming and JavaScript sites, and special effects/Java utilities. See the Web Sites area for examples of Java use on the Web. You can also search for specific information on Gamelan; a "Windows NT" query produced results that included links to Windows-specific Java help files, development environments, and utility files.

The Java Companion (`http://www.xs4all.nl/~dgb/java.html`) is a nice collection of links to Java information from Sun Microsystems' main Java sites, including white papers and technical overviews and in-depth programming information (Fig. 6.4). There are also links to major companies providing Java browsers and development environments, and a short list of Java resources on the Net. This is a well laid out snapshot of the best Web sites related to Java that can get you straight to the relevant information.

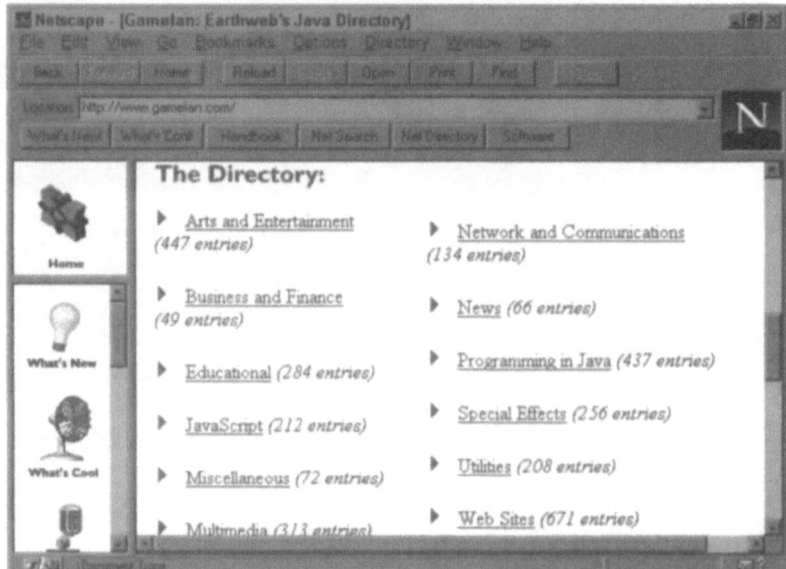

FIGURE 6.3.
Gamelan.

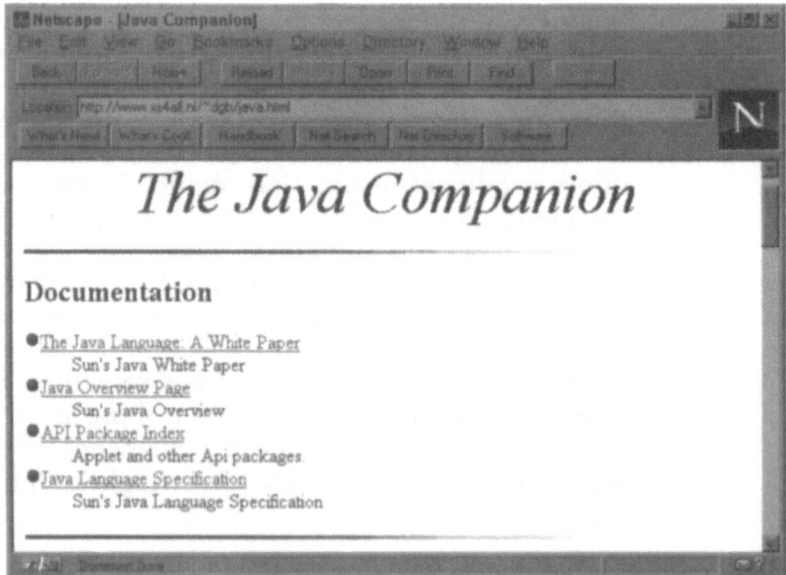

FIGURE 6.4.
Java Companion.

Java has many electronic mailing lists and Usenet newsgroup discussion groups devoted to it. The problem is that the large amount of information flow in them can be hard to handle. Digital Espresso (http://www.io.org/~mentor/DigitalEspresso.html) is a weekly digest of the relevant message traffic, arranged in specific categories (announcements, discussions, bugs and warnings, comments, new applets, services, and products), and edited with a firm hand. There are also help wanted and contact requests sections. The message lists and newsgroups are an important forum for discussing cutting-edge Java technology and development issues related to it, and a news digest is a good way to keep track of current information.

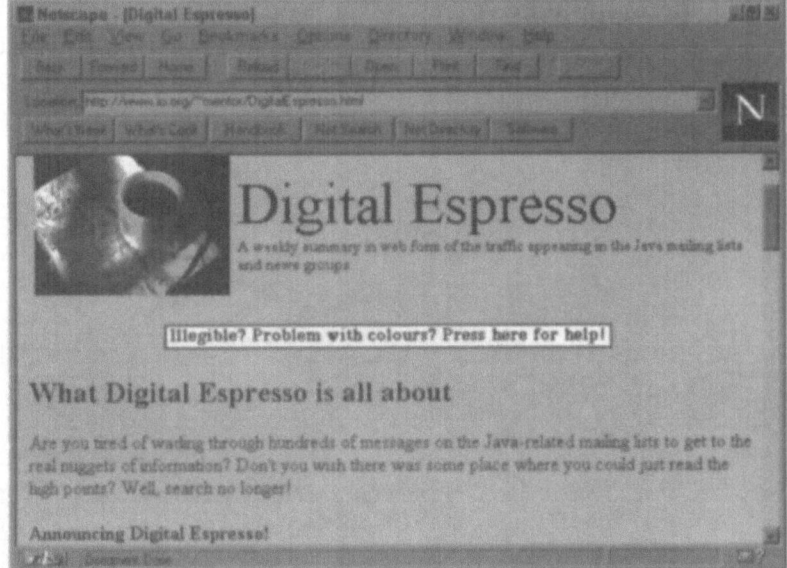

FIGURE 6.5.
Digital Espresso.

Java Development

Java development on NT provides an alternative to developing on Unix systems (although you can do basic Java development on any system with a text editor). The Java IDEs for Windows NT include front ends to Sun's largely text-based Java Development Kit, as well as specific Java development tools from companies like Dimension X and Symantec.

The first place to start with Java development is with the Java Development Kit, from JavaSoft (http://java.sun.com/). The JDK consists of the basic tools you need to develop Java applications, including a Java editor, compiler, and interpreter, and a Java Applet Viewer. Many of the following IDEs discussed work directly from Sun's JDK, and you'll have to download it first before you try any Java programming. The JavaSoft site also provides a wealth of information for the JDK, including technical documentation, programming overviews, and a FAQ.

Sun Microsystems' SunSoft is one of the companies that is now providing a front end to the JDK, with its own Java Workshop product (`http://www.sun.com/sunsoft/Developer-products/java/`), written in Java itself. The toolset includes an integrated project manager, source editor, debugger, and applet viewer. The Java Workshop GUI works in a standard Web browser format, which makes switching between tools easier. The Web site includes product overviews, technical information, and downloading information (for Beta versions). You can also try an interactive demo of the Java Workshop from the site (for Java-enabled browsers only).

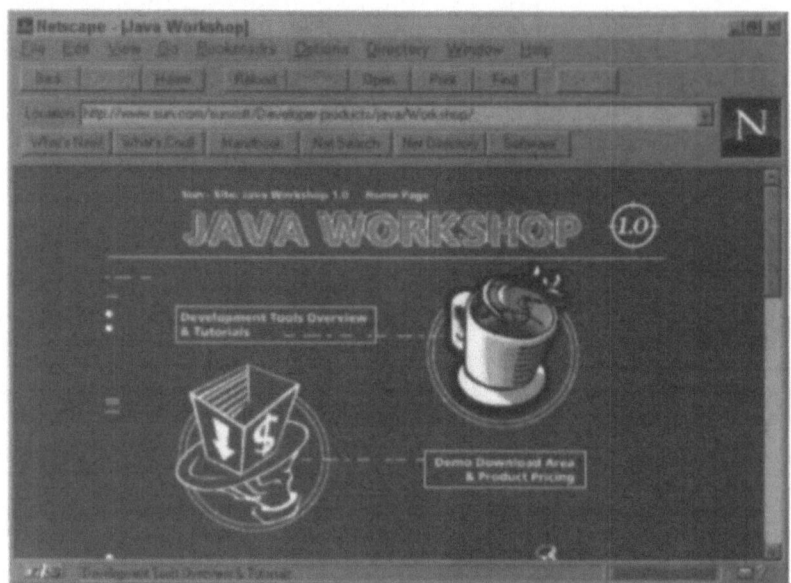

FIGURE 6.6.
Java Workshop.

Netscape's JavaScript Web page (`http://www.netscape.com/comprod/products/navigator/version_2.0/script/`) will fill you in on the efforts to create an easier-to-use Java development system. The site includes a JavaScript Authoring Guide, with information on the basics of using JavaScript for Netscape Navigator scripting, including alternate uses like independent Java windows and frames. There's also a good guide to Java language concepts (values and expressions, object models, and Java-specific statements), and a Reference section (for learning more about terms and special development methods under Java). See the Reference page for specific examples of JavaScript in action, including dynamic calculators, games, and an on-line Federal income tax form that figures out how much you owe. This page also features a good set of links to information and tutorials on JavaScript from across the Net.

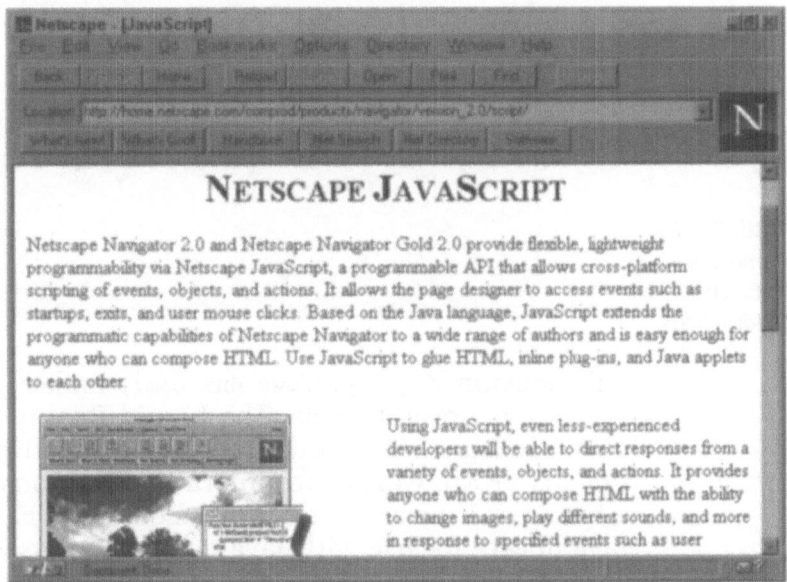

FIGURE 6.7.
JavaScript.

The Perpetually Unfinished Java Guides Page (http://ugweb.cs. ualberta.ca/~nelson/java/JavaTutorial.html) will help you to understand concepts like the Abstract Window ToolKit, a major part of using Java as an interface for Web applets and beyond. This standard is what will enable stand-alone Java applications, and it will be a big part of how Java will be used in the future (in operating systems from Sun, Microsoft, Apple, and others). This site has a good introduction to AWT, an interactive tutorial on the same subject, and many good links to Java-related information.

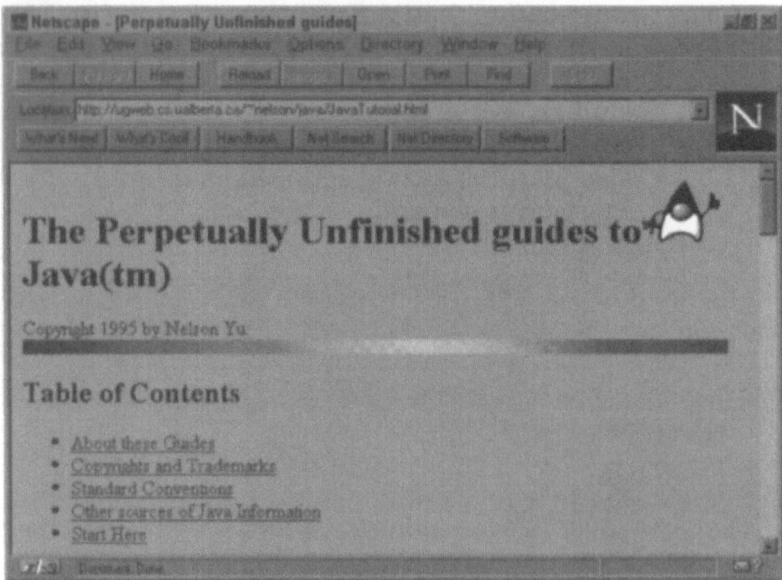

FIGURE 6.8.
Perpetually
Unfinished Java
Guides page.

Dimension X (`http://www.dnx.com/`) makes Java tools for developers at several levels. The Liquid Reality product is a software package that includes tools for embedding Java applets inside 3D VRML worlds (for interactive motion effects), as well as a browser. It works with Dimension X's ICE, an integrated 3D Java library for use with Java-enabled browsers. Liquid Motion is an application that creates Java animations with an easy-to-use Windows menu system. It generates Java code automatically, and requires no programming skills to achieve impressive Java effects.

Soft As It Gets ED for Windows, The Java IDE (Integrated Development Environment) (`http://www.ozemail.com.au/~saig`) provides a standardized Java development application. The ED Java IDE features a hierarchical class browser, Java compiler support, and automatic launching of standard Java tools. The Web site features a downloadable trial version that includes a simple tutorial, Creating Your First Java Program.

The Paradigm Exchange Grinder JDE (`http://www.tpex.com/`) is a Java Development Environment for Windows (Fig. 6.11). It consists of a GUI front end to the text-based Java development tools from Sun. The JDE includes an integrated Java editor, a class browser, applet testing software, and links to the Java compiler and debugger. The Web site features product overviews and links to trial versions of Grinder that you can download.

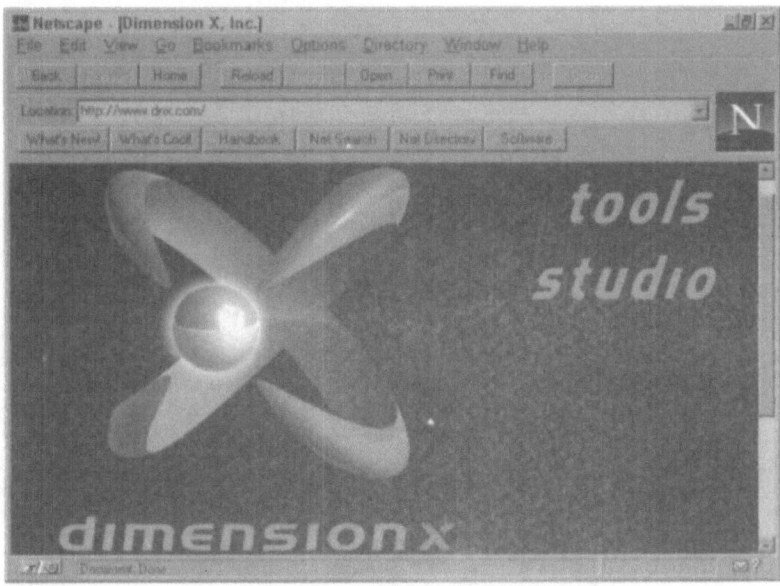

FIGURE 6.9.
Dimension X.

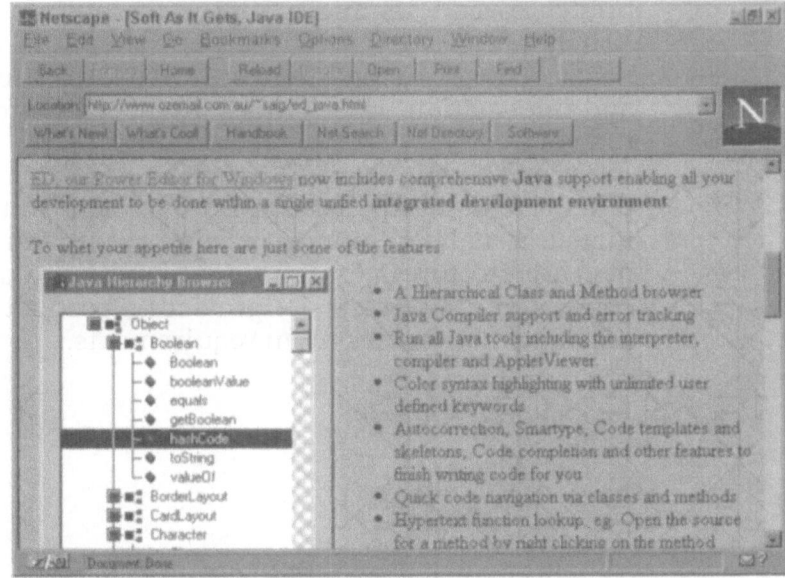

FIGURE 6.10.
ED Java IDE.

FIGURE 6.11.
Paradigm Exchange
Grinder.

Symantec's (`http://www.symantec.com/`) Java development software is centered around Cafe, a visual Java development and debugging system for Windows NT. Cafe supports Web page applet and stand-alone Java application creation, and features visual design and project management tools, class and hierarchical browsers, and an integrated compiler. The Web site features product overviews and on-line ordering information for Cafe. You can also check out Java Central, a section that features a good collection of links to Java-related Web sites and Java books, and information on electronic mailing lists for Symantec customers.

Borland's Latte (`http://www.borland.com/`) is a graphical Windows NT Rapid Application Development suite for Java. It features a visual development environment with reusable component architecture, a Java-optimized toolset, and built-in database connectivity. The Web site provides a product overview, a FAQ, and information on system requirements.

FIGURE 6.12.
Symantec
JavaCentral.

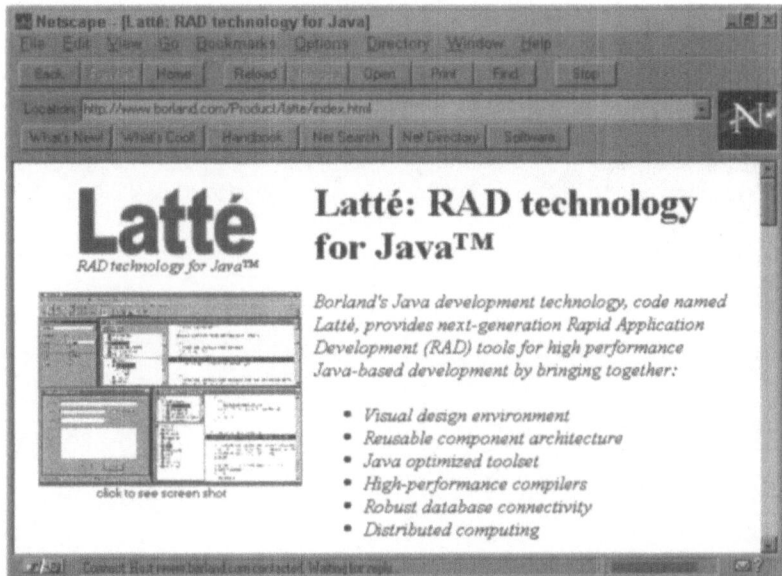

FIGURE 6.13.
Borland Latte.

7
Virtual Reality and VRML for NT

Virtual reality (VR) and the future of the Web are tied closely to the increases in system performance that software like Windows NT can provide. The dream is to interact with others in a different mode than the Email interface that is most common to computer users today. VR will introduce the idea of 3D representation to the Web. This will include Web sites with 3D models of objects for sale (a car you can inspect from several angles, for example), interactive walkthroughs of virtual shopping malls and amusement parks, and even interactive meeting places that will provide you with a 3D representation of yourself that you can inhabit from your computer.

The path to this dream is connected to the Web via VRML, the Virtual Reality Modeling Language. VRML developed as an extension to the HTML Web page creation standard. It's a specialized way to describe three-dimensional scenes that can operate over the Internet, including architectural walkthroughs, interactive art galleries, and virtual cities. Stand-alone software and/or specialized extensions to Web browsers are needed to view VRML files. These programs and extensions typically provide extra controls for moving about a scene (walking through a virtual office building by using a forward arrow to go through it, for example, or for rotating, panning, and swiveling a 3D model around).

Extensions to VRML also allow specialized representations of characters in a given setting, including yourself. With specialized software, you can connect to Web sites that feature "rooms" with characters that are other users connected to the site at the same time. You interact with these characters in a way that is modeled after the real world (i.e., you move closer to a person to engage them in conversation), and you can select/create your own character representation (it's actually a 3D rendering file). An example of how this technology is being used is a virtual chat room, where users can move toward each other and interact in real time.

VRML and its extensions are exciting Web technology, but they add a large overhead to your system. Rendering 3D models on the fly can be a drain on your resources, which is where Windows NT comes in. On the PC platform, it's probably the best (non-Unix) operating system for VRML, due to its advanced multithreading architecture and sophisticated graphics support. NT includes the GL graphics subsystem, a specialized set of graphic routines that can be used by developers to make more efficient VRML programs. The GL standard works across high-end Unix workstations to Windows NT, and it's a good idea to look for VRML browsers that support it under NT. Of course, it also helps to have a fast processor, lots of RAM, and a good PCI/Local Bus video card for maximum performance.

The following software and related Web sites reviewed include NT-capable VRML browsers, Netscape and Microsoft Explorer VRML plug-ins, and virtual environment software. It's relatively easy to add VRML to your NT Web browsing environment, and the sites provide downloading instructions and sample models and worlds that you can explore.

VRML Viewers and Related Software for NT

Netscape's Live3D (http://home.netscape.com/comprod/products/navigator/live3d/) add-in provides VRML compatibility (by placing VRML motion buttons inside your Web browser window), and also adds advances like live media support (ShockWave animations, VDOLive video, and RealAudio sound inside 3D spaces). Live3D was developed from Paper Software's WebFX VRML software product, and it's based on the proposed Moving Worlds VRML 2.0 standard. It also includes developer support for Java extensions, and you'll be able to develop and interact with Java applets inside 3D scenes. See the Netscape Live3D Web site for a good overview of the software, and links to downloading directories, VRML resources, press releases, and Live3D examples. Netscape plans to integrate Live3D into a future release of Netscape Navigator, and you can start on the ground floor here.

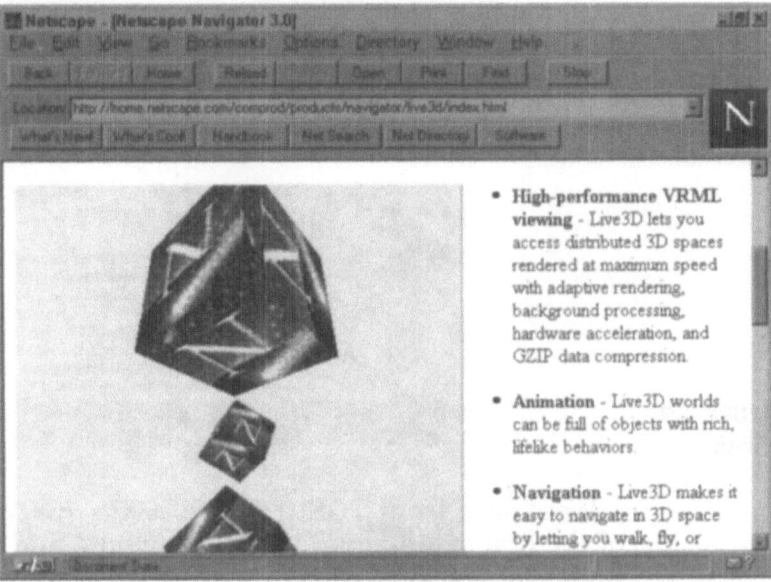

FIGURE 7.1.
Live3D.

Paper Software's WebFX VRML browser plug-in is now becoming Live3D, as described above. Their Web site (http://www.paperinc.com/) features the same Live3D links, and also includes some of the coolest VRML worlds you can browse and explore, and lots of good VRML information.

WIRL, from VREAM (http://www.vream.com/), is a popular Netscape 2.0 VRML plug-in. It supports JAVA and VREAM's own in line VRML script extensions (Fig. 7.2). There is also good support for Microsoft's RealityLab rendering mechanism, video card acceleration, and sophisticated rendering techniques (like shading and texture wrapping). See the Web site for links to cool demo software, press releases, FAQs, and background information. There's also a great set of 3D demos to cruise through, and links to other companies' VRML sites.

Integrated Data Systems (http://www.ids-net.com/ids/) offers V.Realm, a Windows NT compatible VRML browser that's available either as a Netscape plug-in or as a stand-alone Web application. It supports its own rendering subsystems and VRML behavior extensions, as well as "point and jump" navigation and navigational bookmarking. The Web site has links to on-line user manuals, customer information, and product descriptions, as well as cool VRML words and cities to interact with.

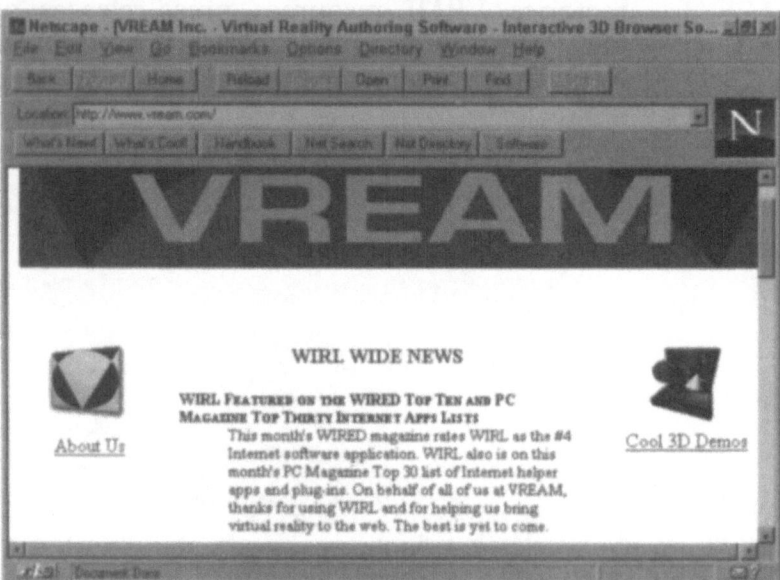

FIGURE 7.2.
VREAM.

WebSpace from TGS (http://www.tgs.com/WebSpace/) was one of the first stand-alone VRML browsers, and the company continues to develop VRML browsing software and standards with some of the hottest VRML companies in the business. WebSpace is available for Windows NT on the Intel and MIPS platform, with support for Alpha and PowerPC to soon follow. See the Web site for press releases, developer information, on-line user guides/FAQs, and a small TGS Holodeck VRML sampler.

Chaco Communications (http://www.chaco.com/) provides an NT VRML 1.0 external viewer, VRScout, that's also available as a Web browser plug-in. The software provides a high level of functionality with standard VRML, and uses specialized graphics routines (from Intel and Microsoft) to enhance performance. You might also be interested in Pueblo, Chaco's MUD (multiuser domain) software that works over the Web. It provides a 3D community experience, and supports VRML with specialized extensions, and Netscape plug-ins (like Shockwave and Real Audio) inside the 3D scenes. Chaco's site provides a good level of information on the VRScout and Pueblo products, including press releases, product backgrounders and help files, and downloading instructions. There are also links to MUD worlds and VRML scenes you can check out yourself.

WorldView, from Intervista (http://www.webmaster.com/vrml/), is another Windows-NT compatible VRML browser. It's currently a stand-alone application, with development of a Web browser plug-in to follow. Its special features include graphics acceler-

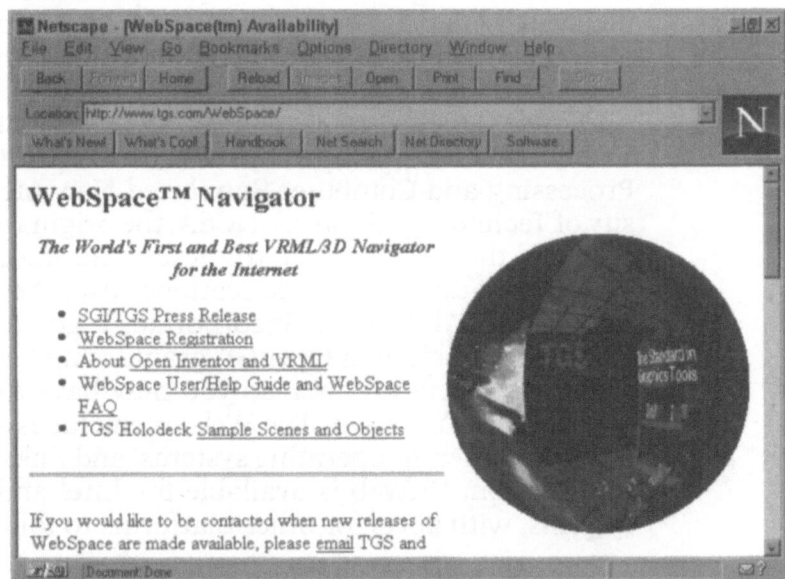

FIGURE 7.3.
WebSpace.

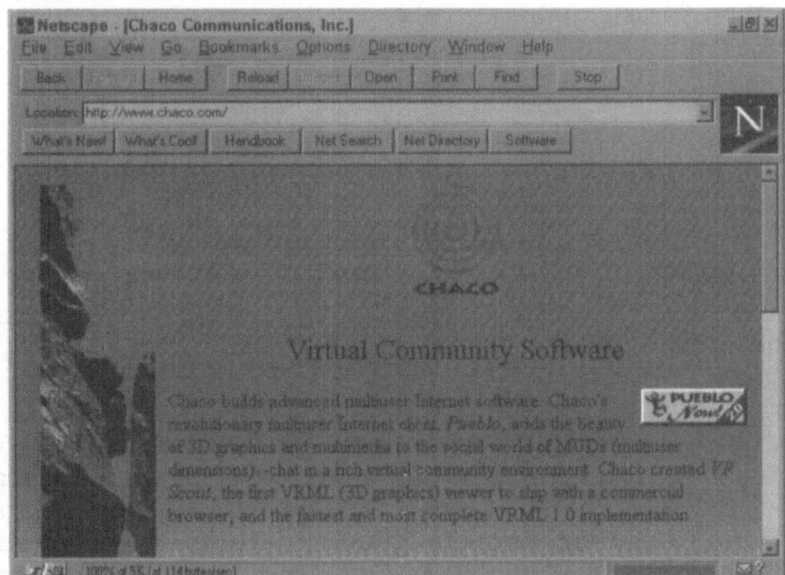

FIGURE 7.4.
Chaco/VRScout.

ation (using Microsoft's RealityLab software), easy-to-use controls, and configurable camera viewpoints. The Web site has an illustrated Guided Tour of the WorldView software and its various components, as well as general installation information and FAQs, and links to a small collection of VRML test files.

VRWeb (http://hgiicm.tu-graz.ac.at:80/9CAF025D/Cvrweb) is a VRML browser developed by IICM (the Institute for Information Processing and Computer-Supported New Media, Graz University of Technology, Austria), NCSA, the original developers of Mosaic, and the University of Minnesota, the developers of Gopher. This public-domain (for educational use; the software is copyrighted) VRML browser incorporates a good level of advanced technology, including OpenGL graphics and VRML with extensions. It's a beta product, so you may have to be careful in installing and running it. The Web site includes installation notes, FAQs for different operating systems, and links to general VRML information. VRWeb is available for Intel and Alpha-based NT systems, with ports for other platforms to follow.

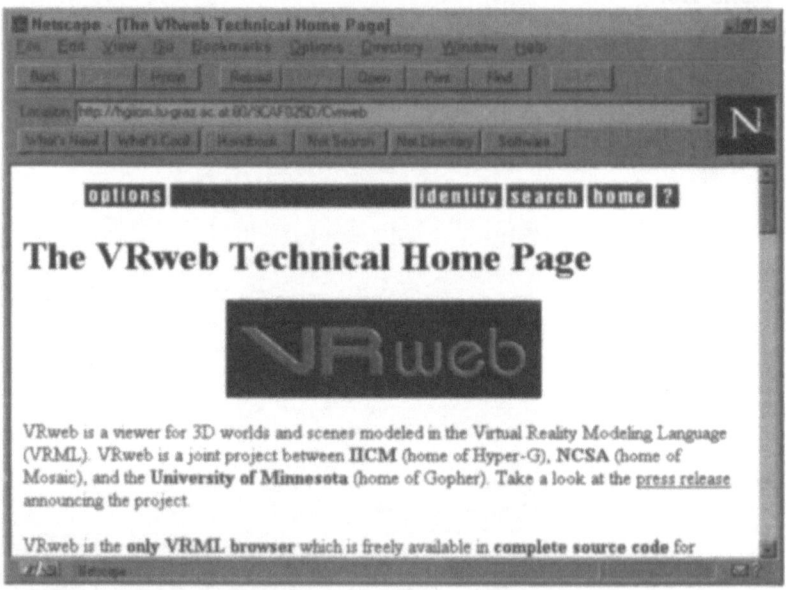

FIGURE 7.5.
VRWeb.

DIVE Labs' Amber VRML browser (http://www.divelabs.com/vrml.htm) is a stand-alone NT shareware application used to view VRML files over the Net. It supports OpenGL and sophisticated rendering techniques, and works with interesting VR hardware, like Virtual I/O's i-glasses head-mounted display and the 5DT data glove. The site includes a read-me file for more information, and an overview of how the product works. The Amber VRML browser is currently for Intel-based NT systems only, but check the Web site for new releases.

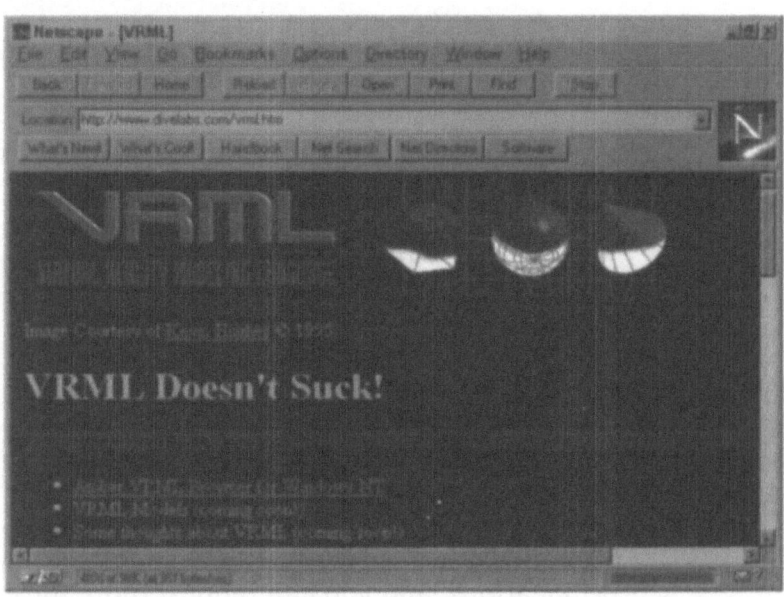

FIGURE 7.6.
Amber.

Black Sun's CyberGate (http://www2.blacksun.com/beta/) is a virtual-environment simulator that lets you interact with representations of other users with your own 3D "persona." CyberGate works with Netscape Navigator and Internet Explorer, and includes custom navigation tools to help you move through VRML spaces. The Web site features information on the software, including system requirements (it currently runs on Intel-based NT systems), release notes, and downloading instructions. There are also press releases, technical white papers, and links to virtual worlds you can explore.

GLView (http://www.snafu.de/~hg/) is an advanced 3D Viewer/ VRML browser for Windows NT that takes good advantage of the OpenGL graphics subsystem. It allows NT users to browse VRML worlds and import 3D rendering models in a variety of formats. It also supports VRML 2.0 extensions, including some interesting Java-related applications. See the Web site for more information, including product data sheets, downloading and installation instructions, and links to cool demos. There's also a good set of links to VRML and VRML-related Web sites across the Internet.

NeTpower's Vizia 3D Viewer (http://webber.netpower.com/pages /products/vizia.htm) is primarily for viewing and embedding 3D models in OLE 2.0-compliant documents, but can also view VRML files from across the Internet. There's some background

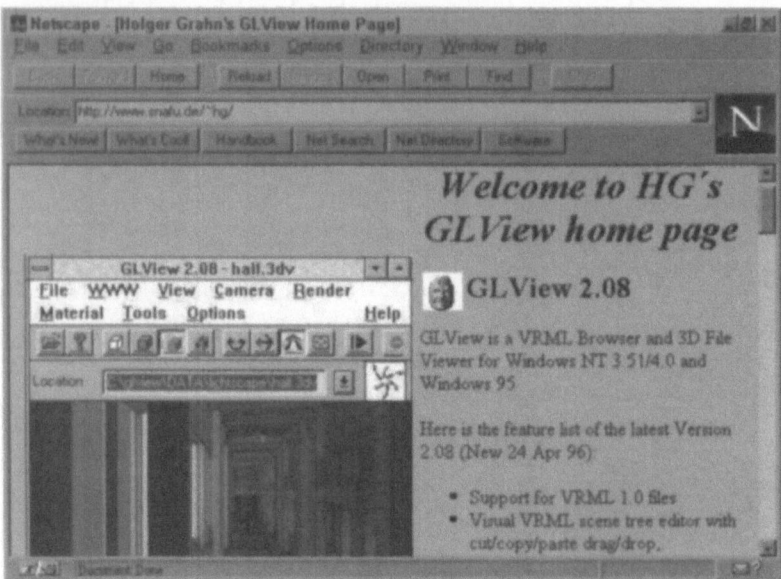

FIGURE 7.7.
GLView.

information on Vizia at the NeTpower site, including technical specifications, and you can request more information via an on-line form. Vizia is available for Intel, MIPS, and Alpha NT platforms.

The TerraForm VRML Browser from Brilliance Labs (http://www.brlabs.com/) is a VRML browser that is designed to work especially well with Internet Explorer and future technology coming from Microsoft. It supports Microsoft's "Sweeper" technology to ensure network reliability, and uses the Intel 3DR graphics subsystem to accelerate VRML rendering on Pentium systems. TerraForm also works with Netscape 2.0, and can be downloaded as a stand-alone VRML application or as a browser plug-in. Brilliance Labs intends to support Microsoft's ActiveVRML standard for advanced VRML, and its NT VRML browsers should bear watching.

Topper, from Autodesk's Kinetix multimedia division (http://www.ktx.com/products/hyperwire/download.htm), is a Netscape 2.0-compatible VRML plug-in that allows you to navigate and view extended VRML scenes. It supports VRBL, Kinetix's Virtual Reality Behavior Language, which allows animation and behavioral effects to be used in VRML. Topper can also be used to view 3D Studio .3DS and AutoCAD .DXF file formats. The Kinetix site includes information on Hyperwire, the Java development environment that can be used to create enhanced VRML worlds, including technical papers and general background information. See the downloading page at the Hyperwire site for more infor-

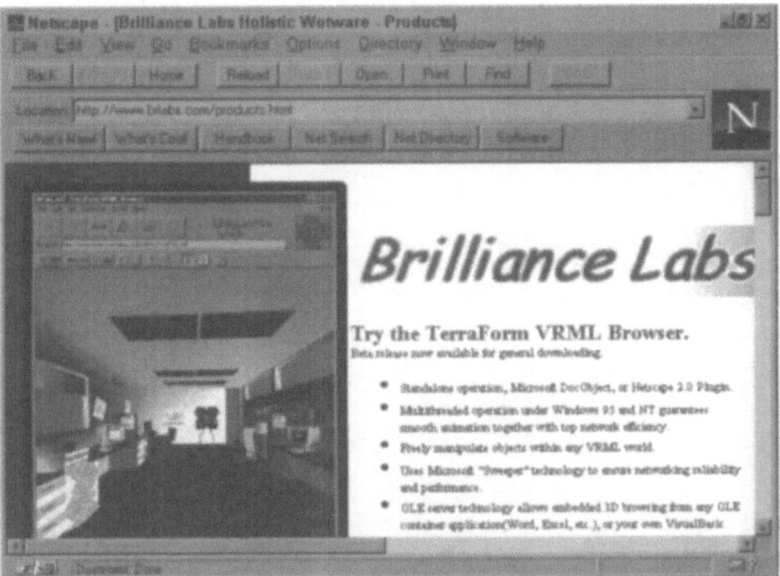

FIGURE 7.8.
TerraForm.

mation on Topper, including system requirements.

VRML Express from ModelWorks Software (http://www. modelworks.com/express/) is an Integrated Design Environment for VRML creation, not a VRML browser. This software includes specific editors for Java and VRML, and it supports VRML 1.0, with a skeleton release of Java-enabled VRML support (the proposed VRML 2.0 "Moving Worlds" specification). The Web site also includes a FAQ with more specific information, downloadable screen shots of Express in action, and links to VRML and Java information sites.

MemeViewer, from Immersive Systems (http://www.immersive. com/), is a 3D environment simulator, not unlike a VRML browser (Fig. 7.9). It's based on MEME, the Multitasking Extensible Messaging Environment specification. It allows browsing and interaction with advanced 3D scenes that are in the MEME format. You can download a copy of the stand-alone application, which runs on Intel-based Windows NT systems. The Immersive site has more information on programming MEME, including technical papers, and sample MEME worlds to explore.

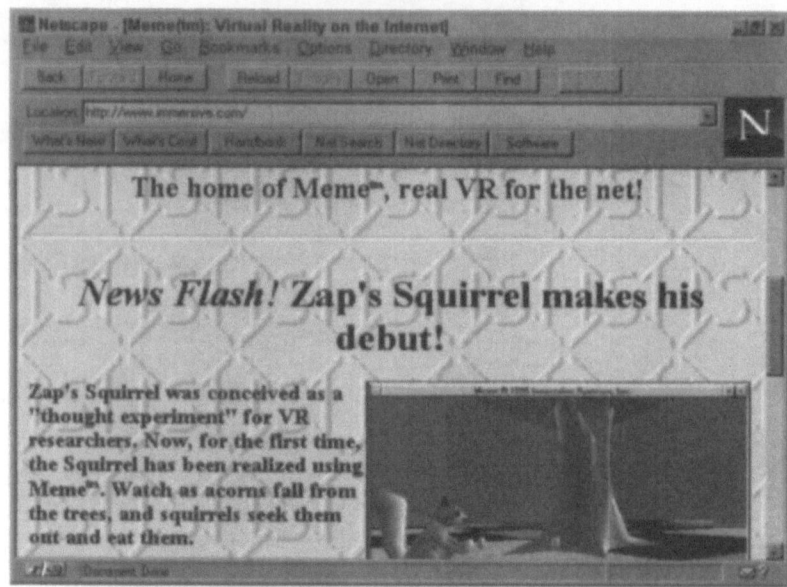

FIGURE 7.9.
MemeViewer.

Intel's Camino Moondo browser (http://ruatha.icon.portland.
or.us/moondo/docs/) is a environment simulator that allows Web
users to enter and participate in 3D virtual worlds with live characters. You can create your own custom "avatar" and use it to
interact with other Moondo users. The Web site includes information on the Moondo standard, and overviews of the Camino
client (a stand-alone NT Web browser for use with .MDO Moondo
Web files) and the Mundo Moondo server, with links to downloading sites, FAQs, tutorials, and cool Moondo sites.

Sony's CyberPassage (http://sonypic.com/VS-E/works/browser/
what.html) is a VRML 2.0-compliant browser that works as a
Netscape 2.0 (or greater) plug-in. It includes support for VRML
and texture files, as well as audio file playback. The CyberPassage
2.0 release is compatible with the Moving Worlds VRML 2.0 standards, and includes enhanced VRML features. Starting with NT
4.0, you can use DirectX with CyberPassage. DirectX includes increased functionality for sound and video hardware when used
with NT 4.0 and the appropriate hardware and software. See
Sony's Virtual Society on the Web site for more information, including system requirements, downloading and installation instructions, technical information, and sample VRML files you
can try out.

FIGURE 7.10.
Camino-Moondo.

CyberTerm (`http://wattle.itd.adelaide.edu.au/~snoswell/ct.html`) is an interesting concept in virtual world simulation software (Fig. 7.11). It is a combination operating system and navigation mechanism that uses a communal setting to explore virtual worlds and collections of Web sites. The software will be originally designed for Windows 3.1 and Windows 95, but should probably be ported to Windows NT in the near future. See the CyberTerm Web site for more information, including technical specs, release schedules, and interesting screenshots.

Silicon Graphics' CosmoPlayer (`http://vrml.sgi.com`) is a VRML 2.0-compliant virtual reality browser for NT (Fig. 7.12). It is based on the Moving Worlds VRML 2.0 standard. The SGI VRML site also includes information on the WebSpace VRML authoring software, and a great index of VR sites in areas like architecture, commerce, geography, history, on-line cities, and entertainment.

Microsoft's ActiveVRML is another advanced VRML standard that will use Active X to embed VRML controls in Microsoft Explorer and other Web browsers. You can find out more about it at the ActiveVRML developer's site (`http://www.microsoft.com/INTDEV/avr/avrml.htm`), which includes a tutorial with in-line examples, and information on system requirements.

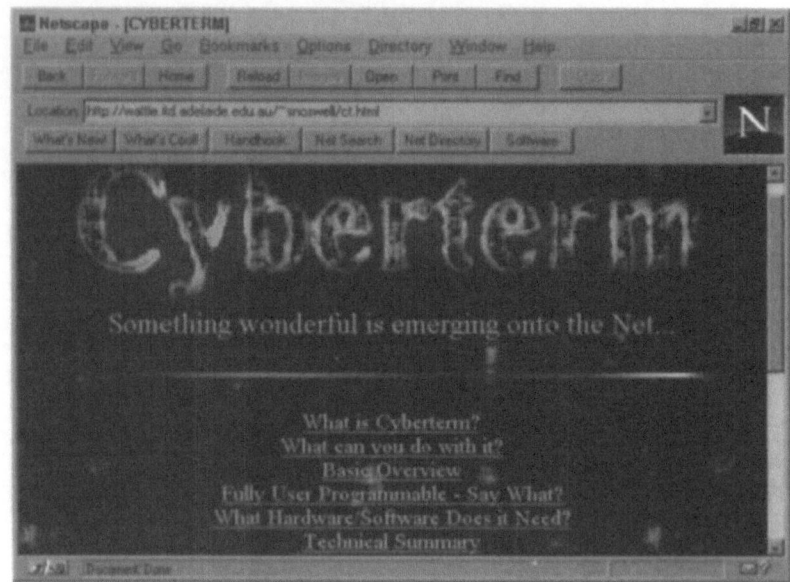

FIGURE 7.11.
CyberTerm.

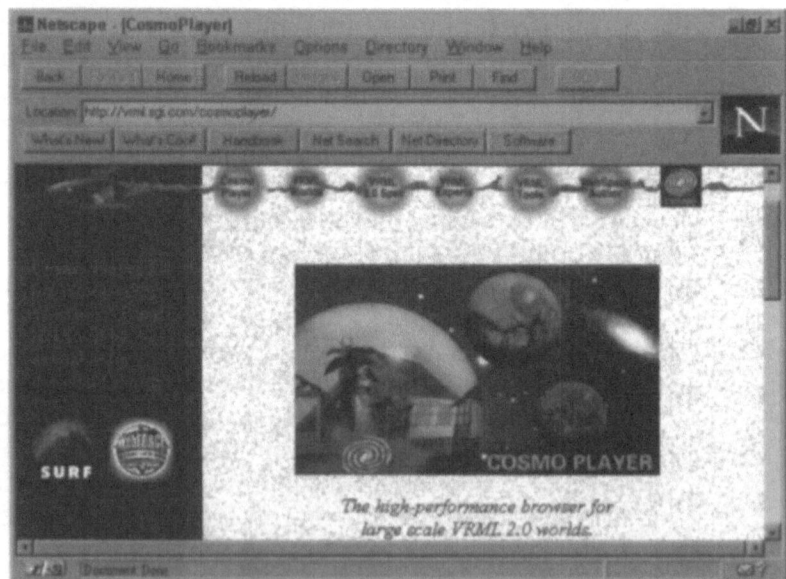

FIGURE 7.12.
Cosmo information.

VRML and Virtual Reality Information Centers on the Net

On The Net: Internet Resources in Virtual Reality (http://www. hitl.washington.edu/projects/knowledge_base/onthenet.html) is a categorical collection of VR sites on the Web, including documentation, software, VRML demos, and personalities in VR.

The VRML Repository at the San Diego Supercomputing Center (http://rosebud.sdsc.edu/vrml/) is a collection of VRML documents and links to related sites. It's an interesting collection of information on VR.

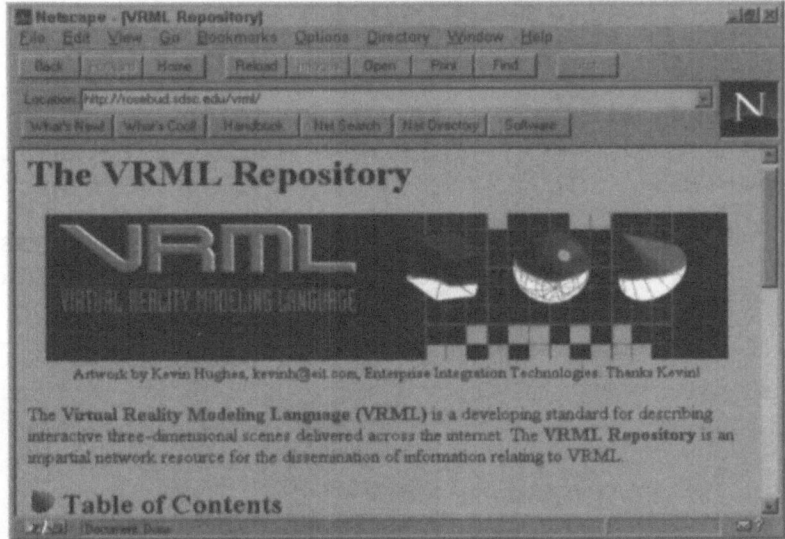

FIGURE 7.13.
VRML Repository.

The VRML Quick Reference from NASA will give a good overview of the main VRML terms and concepts. You can find it at http://coney.hq.nasa.gov/vrml/vrml.html.

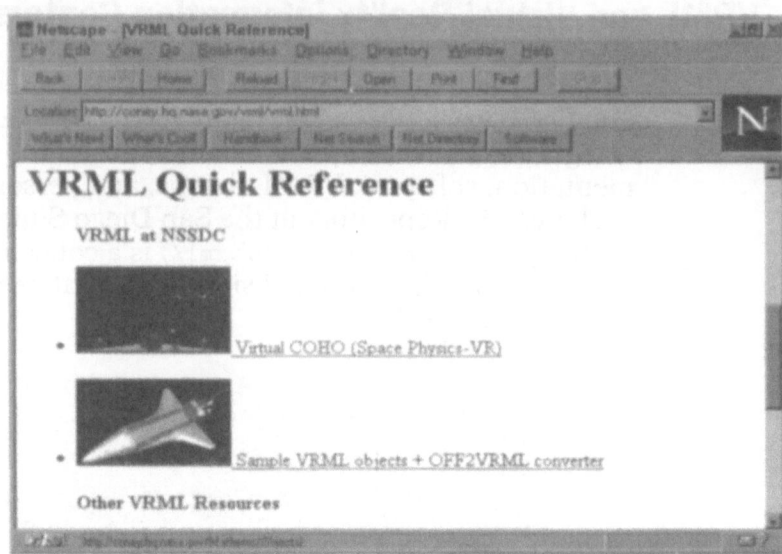

FIGURE 7.14.
NASA VRML Quick
Reference.

VRASP is an alliance of students and professionals working in VR. You can find out more about the organization and its projects at `http://www.vrasp.org/vrasp/`.

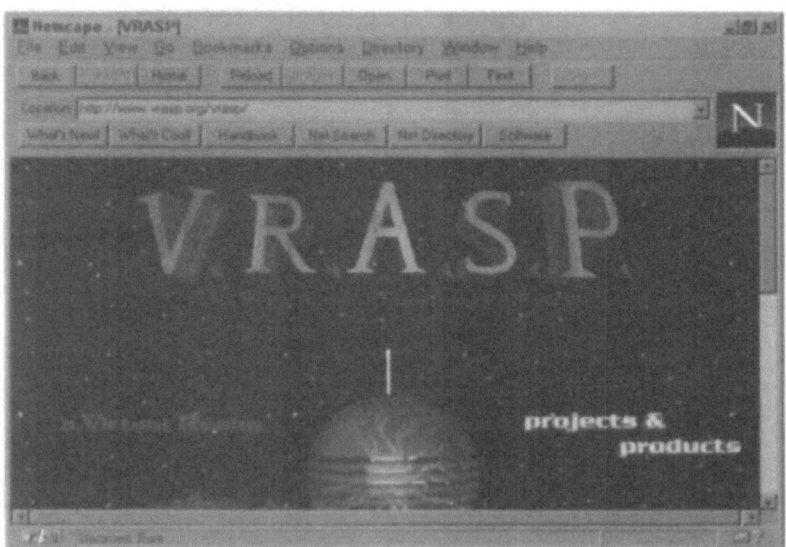

FIGURE 7.15.
VRASP site.

Mesh Mart's VRML and Virtual Reality on the Web (`http://cedar.cic.net/~rtilmann/mm/vrml.htm`) is another subject-oriented VR index, with links to good sites for VR software and hardware, VRML tools, and VR sites.

The VRML Forum (`http://vrml.wired.com/`) is an in-depth connection to the main on-line discussion groups for VR on the Net. This is a good place to pursue your interest in VR and VRML, and to see in what directions it will go in the future.

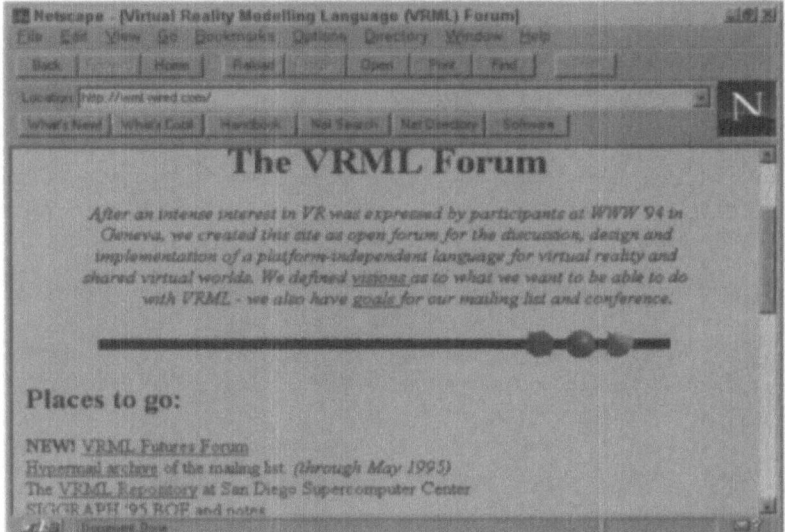

FIGURE 7.16.
VRML Forum.

8
Advanced Web Technologies

NT's advanced features make it one of the first platforms that Web developers target for their new offerings. Web technologies that include advanced multimedia features, object-oriented programming functions, and interactive application communications are just some of the new Web trends that NT is poised to take advantage of in the near future. In turn, being aware of these new technologies gives NT developers and users the ability to integrate richer media formats into their interactive Web sites, and to develop more sophisticated Web applications.

LiveConnect

Netscape's LiveConnect technology (`http://home.netscape.com/comprod/products/navigator/version_3.0/connect/`) links plug-ins, Java applets, Javascript, and HTML code in Web pages. This means that any of these elements can trigger any of the other elements. For example, an embedded video sequence could be synched to a separate audio playback file. A business application could take the form of a Java applet that retrieves stock updates via a live feed, and matches the information to buy/sell orders set via a predesigned HTML form. A Javascript function would then invoke an audio warning and a pop-up dialog box advising the user to buy or sell one's stock, and generate a secure transaction.

Netscape offers a Software Development Kit for LiveConnect;

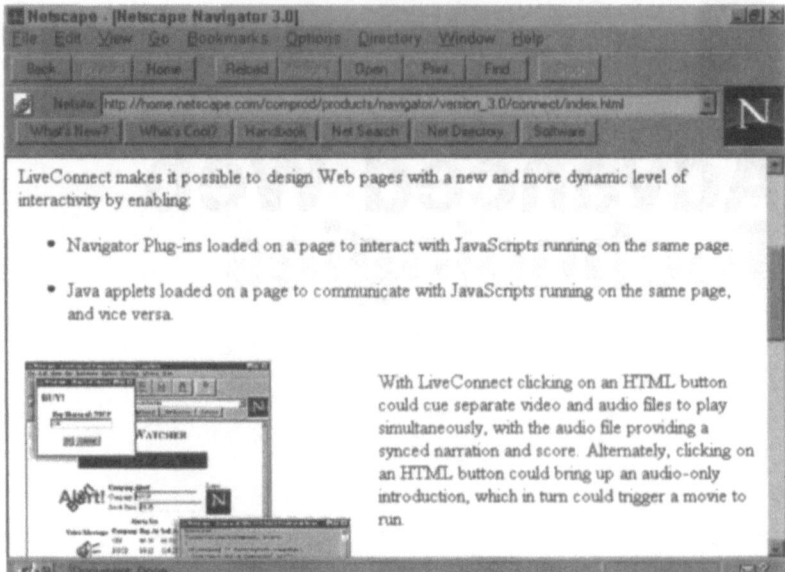

FIGURE 8.1.
LiveConnect.

you can download it at the LiveConnect site mentioned above. The LiveConnect **SDK** features documentation, programming files, and sample code for plug-in development using LiveConnect. There's also an on-line plug-in Development Guide, with sections on general design, information on the steps needed to create a plug-in for the Windows platform, and special Windows issues.

The LiveConnect Showcase features on-line examples of enriched Web sites from companies such as Tumbleweed, Future-Wave, MBed, and NetScene.

The Tumbleweed Envoy plug-in (`http://www.twcorp.com`) brings fully formatted documents to Web pages via Javascript and Java applets; a document created in any application can be displayed in a Web page along with a custom interface and manipulated by Javascript and/or user interactions.

FutureWave's FutureSplash (`http://www.futurewave.com/`) uses LiveConnect to create a multimedia navigation tool, with functions like interactive movie controls and map viewing. Future-Splash buttons and frame actions use JavaScript to control FutureSplash movies, LiveConnect-enabled plug-ins, and Java applets. FutureSplash movies can be controlled via HTML links or another FutureSplash graphic file.

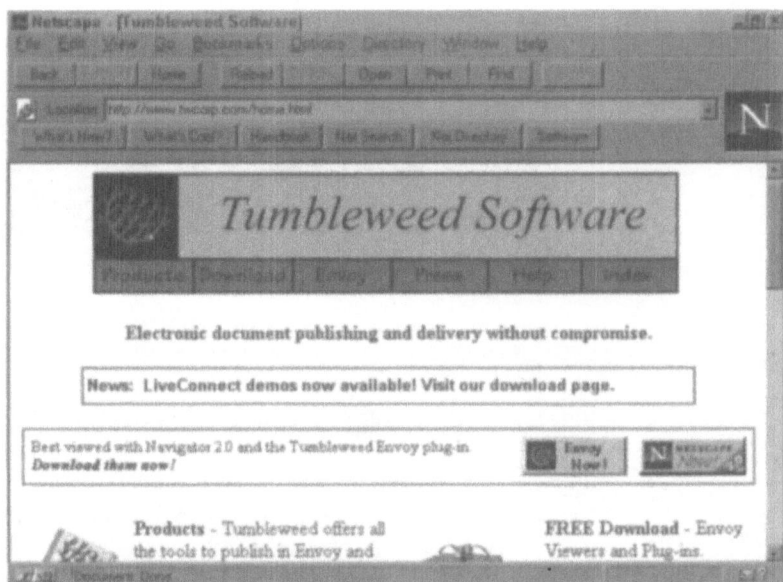

FIGURE 8.2.
Tumbleweed Envoy.

The Bulls and Bears Stock Ticker, from mBed (http://www.mbed. com), is a stock portfolio tracking service (Fig.8.3). It uses Javascript to prompt a Java applet (via LiveConnect) to check a CGI program for update information. It then passes this information to the user via sound and visual alerts. The Ticker runs in the background, and updates are timed at 30-second intervals.

NetScene's PointPlus (http://www.net-scene.com) is an Intranet application that runs a PowerPoint presentation with a customized control panel for user interaction (Fig. 8.4). The control panel is written in Javascript and connects to the PointPlus Plug-In using a Java applet. The applet also allows users to interact with the presentation by adding comments to individual slides using predefined forms that change for each individual slide.

To find out more about how Live Connect's Java integration, check out http://home.netscape.com/comprod/products/navigator/ version_3.0/developer/mojava.html.

Companies supporting Netscape's LiveConnect architecture include Adobe, Aimtech, Autodesk, Dun & Bradstreet Software, Macromedia, and Silicon Graphics.

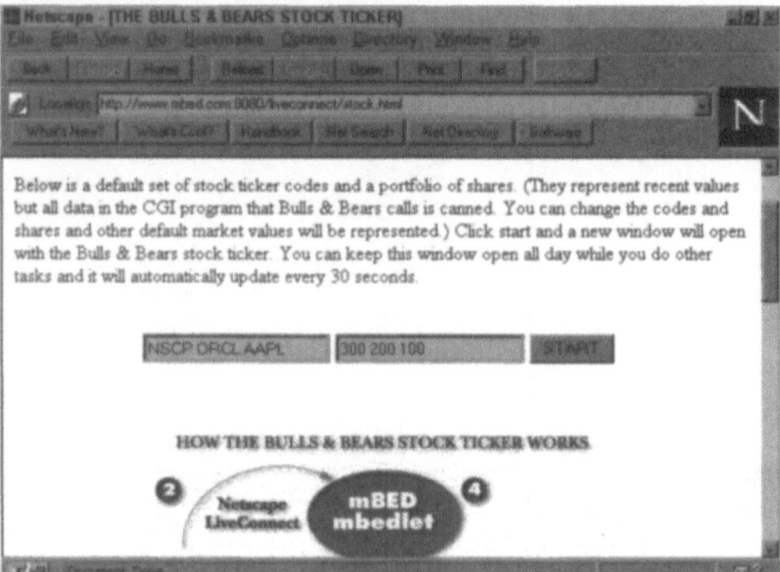

FIGURE 8.3.
mBed Web site.

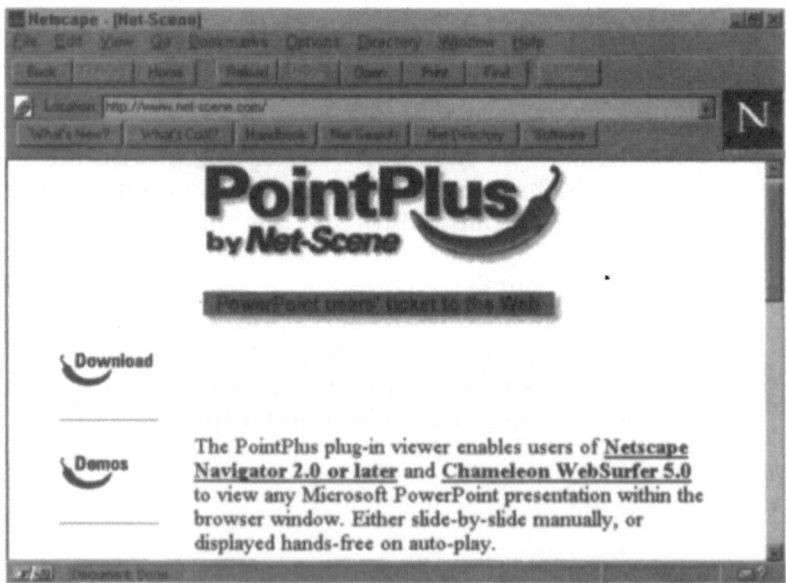

FIGURE 8.4.
PointPlus.

ActiveX

ActiveX, developed by Microsoft and Intel, is an interesting technology that will add significant functionality to Web browsers and server software for NT. It's being developed in several parts: The ActiveX controls are embedded control panels and interactive forms that can be used inside Web pages to access OLE applications. ActiveX documents use the ActiveX controls to read file formats for Microsoft Word, Excel, and PowerPoint directly inside Web browsers. The ActiveX server framework will integrate protocols like HTTP into the Windows NT Server, and add OLE connectivity to the corporate Intranet and the Internet as well. ActiveX will also integrate Java and Visual Basic into its development environment.

Microsoft's Internet Control Pack features ActiveX components for common Web protocols. Developed by Microsoft and Net-Manage, these include ActiveX controls for protocols like Winsock, FTP, HTTP, SMTP, HTML, and HTTP. Developers can include these protocols in custom browsers, Email readers, and file transfer programs, and include these services in applications that they write. You can download it from `http://www.microsoft.com/icp`.

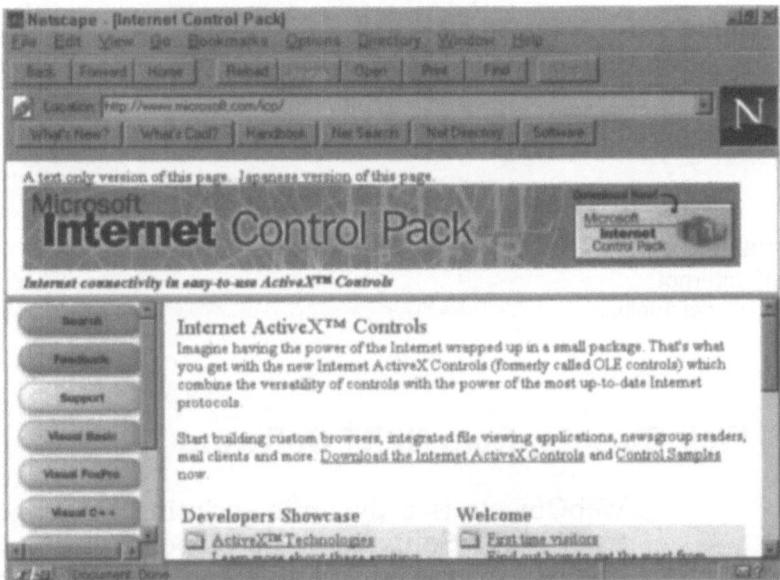

FIGURE 8.5.
MS Internet Control Pack Web site.

You can also look into the ActiveX Development Kit, which includes a Software Development Kit for ActiveX, sample applications, and information on how to integrate Microsoft applications with the ActiveX technology. The ADK also includes custom OS extensions to Windows NT to support the Microsoft Internet Information Server, and a copy of the IIS itself.

Several third-party vendors will be providing custom ActiveX controls for business application development, including Blue Sky Software, Borland, hip communications, Powersoft, and Soft-Quad.

Other vendors climbing on board the ActiveX bandwagon are Adobe, Attachmate, Corel, Digital, FTP Software, Fulcrum, GTE, Macromedia, Micrografx, NCSA, NEC, Oracle, Quarterdeck, Spyglass, Verity, and Wall Data.

To find out more about ActiveX and other Microsoft Internet technologies, try the Microsoft Internet Developer Toolbox site, http://www.microsoft.com/intdev/.

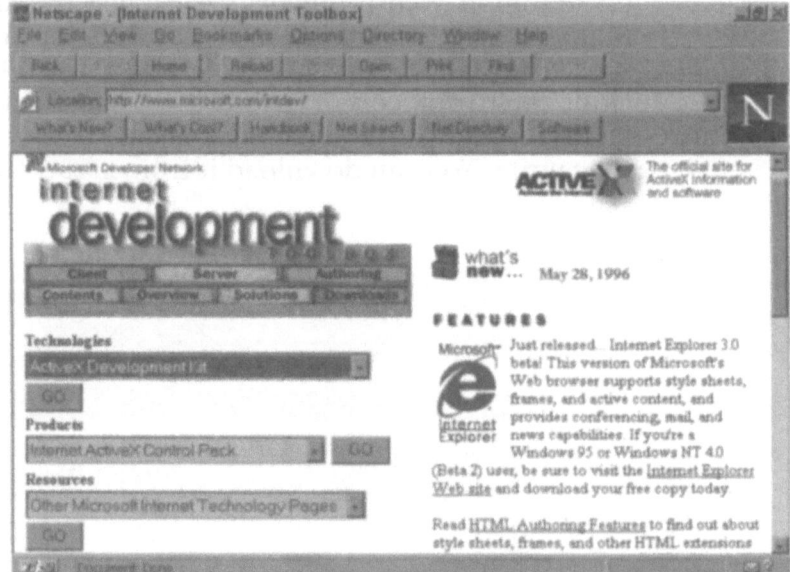

FIGURE 8.6.
MS Internet
Developer Toolbox.

Web Objects, from NeXT Software

WebObjects is a dynamic scripting language for Web servers from NeXT Software. It developed from NextStep, the object-oriented operating system created by Next about 10 years ago. WebObjects, unlike NextStep, is platform-independent; it runs on major operating systems, including Unix variants (from Sun, Digital, Hewlett-Packard, and Next) and Microsoft's Windows NT.

WebObjects comes in three flavors. The base WebObjects Lite software features custom scripts, dynamic HTML, and reusable components. It also supports specialized foundation classes, as well as programming language standards like Java and ActiveX. WebObjects is entirely browser-independent, and will work with standard Windows NT Web server software. You can download the NT version from http://www.next.com for free. It comes with a limited development environment and many useful examples.

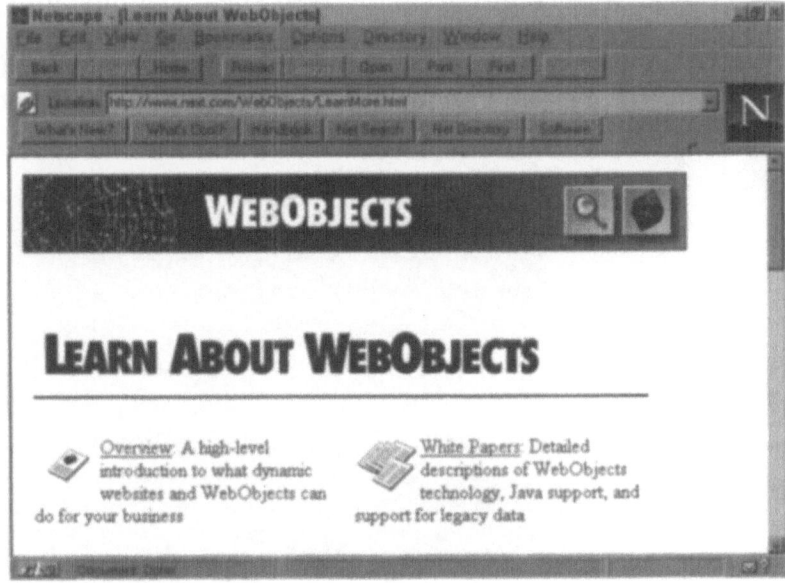

FIGURE 8.7. WebObjects Web site.

The WebObjects Pro product includes the base components as outlined above, as well as scalable application support (this randomly forwards requests to multiple Web servers and performs load distribution). There are also code compilers for C, C++, and Objective C (with Java support in the future), and a distributed objects subsystem, with access to OLE (including OLE Automation servers).

WebObjects Enterprise includes WebObjects Pro's features, as well as Next's Enterprise Objects Framework. EOF provides WebObjects with comprehensive database connectivity tools and a business objects layer that allows the integration of complex business rules inside a Web application.

Next is planning to add a graphical development environment to WebObjects Pro and Enterprise in late 1996. Code-named Tsunami, it will enable users to lay out WebObjects and HTML on each application page, bind the dynamic elements to script methods and variables, and add the server logic components from a graphical interface. It will also allow WebObjects developers to manage the reusable code elements between different WebObjects applications more efficiently.

The examples included with WebObjects are also available online, at `http://www.plsys.co.uk/WebObjects.html`, and `http://www. ped.muni.cz/WebObjects/Examples/ReadMe.html`. You can check them out with any Web browser, even if you don't have WebObjects installed on your system. This is the best way to appreciate what WebObjects can do for your Web site. It works in the background, to allow Web sites a significantly higher degree of functionality and interactivity. The examples include simple interactive applications that explain basic WebObjects concepts, and small versions of interactive browsing and shopping applications that work over the Web.

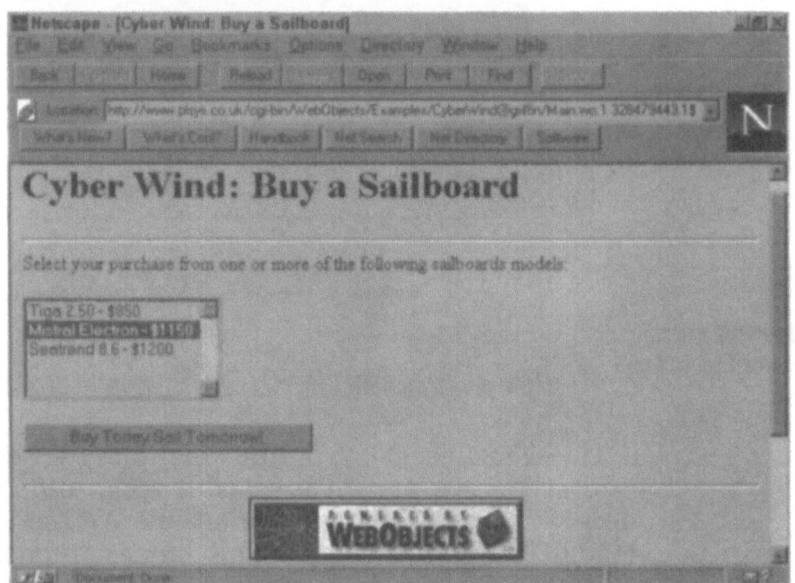

FIGURE 8.8.
A WebObjects
application example.

A more impressive demo can be found on the Web. The Dodge Showroom example (`http://www.next.com/DodgeDemo`) leads to an on-line car showroom. You can select a range of cars to preview by clicking on price information, models, and car types. The WebObjects application builds you a custom Web page with the cars that match your selection. You can also review the cars by changing their color schemes, and use an integrated calculation system to view loan payment information. Other sites using WebObjects for interesting Web applications include Planet Reebok (`http://wofapps2.next.com/cgi-bin/WebObjects/Reebok`) and the Sharper Image (`http://www.sharperimage.com`). Companies planning WebObjects development include Disney, Dreamworks SKG, Fannie Mae, MCI, Merrill Lynch, Mitsubishi, Koyosha, Motorola, and WeatherLabs.

9

The Future of NT: Cairo, Internet, and Intranet Integration

Cairo is the next major release of Windows NT. It will be based on a distributed application framework, using object technologies. The main features will include an improved system interface (already shipping as a part of NT 4.0), a better-integrated file search system, and a sophisticated network viewing system. Cairo will also include easier system administration tools, and a comprehensive integration with Intranets and the World Wide Web. Find out more about it at `http://microsoft.com/ntserver/cairomb.htm` (Fig. 9.1).

Some features of Cairo have already been made available. These include the user interface in Windows 95 and NT 4.0, along with enhancements to the NT Directory Services (NTDS) in Microsoft Exchange Server (better user administration features), and the integration of DCOM (Distributed COM) applications into NT 4.0 via OLE (ActiveX) (Fig. 9.2).

NT Server Cairo will be available in beta in 1997. The Windows NT file system (NTFS) will be upgraded with an object-oriented technology formerly called the Object File System (OFS). This technology gives the file system the ability to store file properties and index system contents. Users will be able to work with files on the local network (and the Internet) more efficiently, including the ability to search for files based on content, not just names and dates. System administrators will also be able to create a logical overview of the NT Server network that will be independent of the physical network.

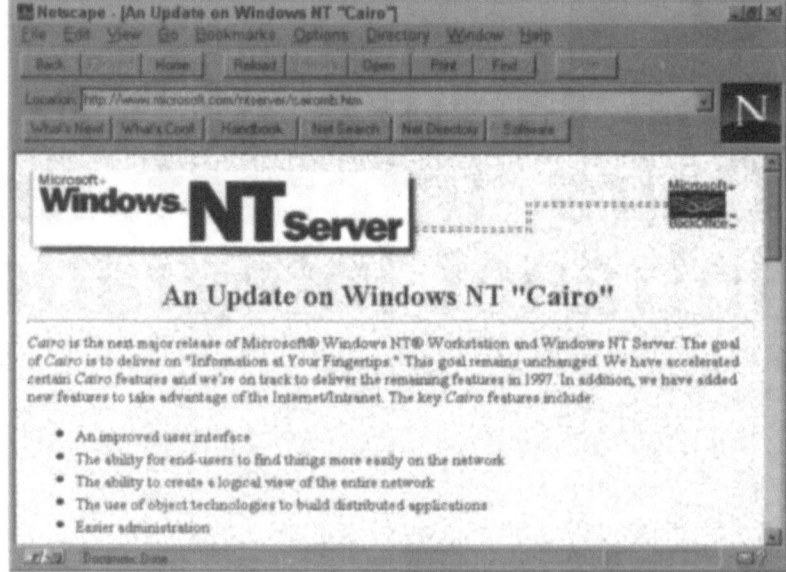

FIGURE 9.1.
Cairo information
page.

FIGURE 9.2.
MS Exchange Server
page.

Cairo will also give applications the ability to access the system directory via a set of consistent APIs (application programming interfaces). Directory Services will support access and management of directory objects, and database access will provide sophisticated query capabilities.

NT Cairo will be integrated with the Internet/Intranet by reorienting its connection with DNS (Domain Name Service), the Internet's way of locating files and resources, to include support for enterprise networks. This will include a gateway between DNS and the Windows Internet name Services (WINS), and the development of dynamic and secure DNS with the IETF (Internet Engineering Task Force).

This Internet-local system directory structure means that the file system will maintain names in the file directory via DNS and Internet domain names, instead of the standard file naming. DNS names, like standard Web addresses (for example, foo.com), will also be the names of Windows NT Cairo file directories, and users will be able to connect to the file system on the Intranet via standard Internet-style protocols. For using the Web, this means that the local NT system will be able to index and search Web servers using the same consistent file navigation system that will be a part of the Cairo OS.

It's also been reported that NT 4.0 (and Cairo) will include an upgrade to the Intel emulator for non-Intel RISC systems, from a 286-based model to a 486. This will improve performance for 16-bit applications. Microsoft also plans to optimize NT for the Intel Pentium Pro architecture.

BackOffice is also expected to be integrated into Cairo's new directory structure. Users will see a common administration interface, and applications will be able to share data transparently. Microsoft is also working to move BackOffice into a more uniform component architecture, and will eliminate redundancies between programs.

You can read about Microsoft's advanced directory structure and Cairo migration plans in a White Paper on the Web, at http:// www.microsoft.com/ntserver/whtpap.htm. This page also has many other interesting papers on NT Server features and Microsoft's future plans for deploying them for Enterprise computing.

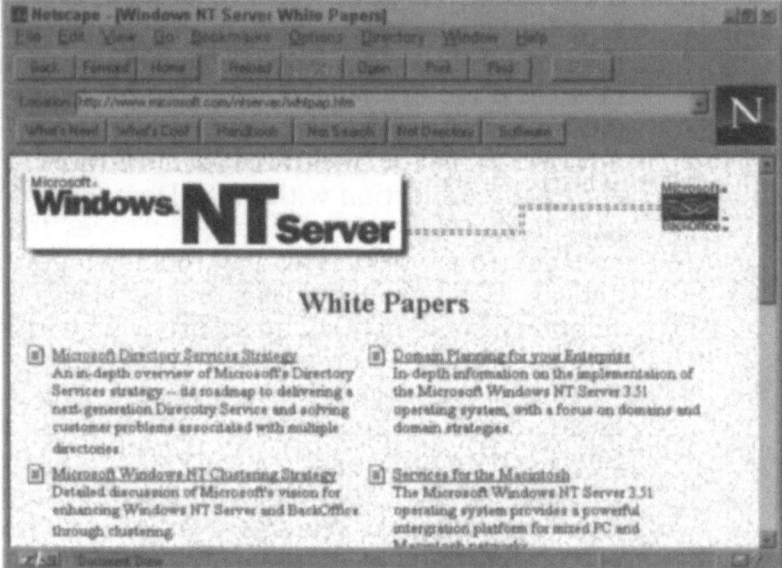

FIGURE 9.3.
MS NT Server White
Papers.

Appendix: Data File Formats on the World Wide Web

The file formats you'll encounter most over the Web include different types of images, animations, and word processing files. You may want to look for utilities to view some of the more esoteric formats at shareware sites on the Net that feature NT-compatible software. See Chapter 4 for more information.

Image File Formats

.GIF Graphics Interchange Format, a standard PC picture file format that Netscape and most other browsers can view directly inside its main window.

.JPG Joint Picture Experts Group compressed image file format that Web browsers can view directly, and can also be viewed using JPEGView externally.

Note: There are a lot of image file formats in use on the Internet that will pertain to certain applications beyond those listed above. You may encounter TIFF images, for example, at some sites. Using a program like LView as a default viewer beyond Netscape's internal capabilities is a good idea (it supports TIFF and PC .BMP file formats), and Photoshop as a further image-handling program for Netscape might also be worth considering.

Motion Video File Formats

.MPG MPEG (Motion Picture Experts Group) video format. Use VMPEG to view MPEG videos and animations properly.

.AVI Video for Windows file format. Netscape Navigator 3.0 can view AVI files directly with the Live Video subsystem, and you can also use the MediaPlayer software that comes with Windows NT as a helper application.

.QT, .MOV QuickTime file formats. PCs need to be configured to use QuickTime properly (look for the software at `http://quicktime.apple.com`). QuickTimeVR files need a QuickTime VR player to run them, also available there.

Compression Formats

.ZIP The standard compression format for PCs. Use WinZip or PKunzip to decompress these files.

.tar UNIX compressed file format (UNIX tar command). Use a shareware tar program to decompress these files.

.gz GNUtar, alternate compressed tar file format (gzip command). Use a GZIP decompression program for these types of files. Note that .gz files are also used for VRML files; most browser VRML helper applications and plug-ins will decode these properly by themselves.

Document File Formats

.TXT Standard ASCII text files (usually README files are in this format). Netscape and most Web browsers will view these types of files directly.

.DOC Microsoft Word document format. Microsoft offers a stand-alone Word document viewer you can download from its Web site.

.WPD WordPerfect document format.

.RTF Rich Text document format, typically with more formatting than ASCII text files.

.PS PostScript file format.

.PDF Adobe Acrobat document format.

Note: As with graphics file formats, there are a lot more document file formats than those mentioned here for more specific word processing programs. It's possible to use plug-in programs to read Microsoft Word or Excel files, or to use a program like MS Word to translate differently formatted files to its own format. Microsoft is developing Active X document support for Internet Explorer 3.0, for direct viewing and interaction with Microsoft Office file formats (Word, Excel, and PowerPoint).

Adobe Acrobat .PDF files need the Acrobat Reader program to view them properly (although native .PDF support is expected in a later version of Netscape, and you can download an in-line Acrobat Reader plug-in). PostScript files on the Internet can be documents, image files, or a combination of both.

Index